blue
rider
press

THE
LEADERLESS
REVOLUTION

THE
LEADERLESS
REVOLUTION

HOW ORDINARY PEOPLE WILL
TAKE POWER AND CHANGE POLITICS
IN THE TWENTY-FIRST CENTURY

CARNE ROSS

BLUE RIDER PRESS
a member of Penguin Group (USA) Inc.
New York

blue
rider
press

Published by the Penguin Group
Penguin Group (USA) Inc., 375 Hudson Street, New York, New York 10014, USA •
Penguin Group (Canada), 90 Eglinton Avenue East, Suite 700, Toronto, Ontario M4P 2Y3,
Canada (a division of Pearson Penguin Canada Inc.) • Penguin Books Ltd, 80 Strand,
London WC2R 0RL, England • Penguin Ireland, 25 St Stephen's Green, Dublin 2, Ireland
(a division of Penguin Books Ltd) • Penguin Group (Australia), 250 Camberwell Road, Camberwell,
Victoria 3124, Australia (a division of Pearson Australia Group Pty Ltd) • Penguin Books India Pvt Ltd,
11 Community Centre, Panchsheel Park, New Delhi–110 017, India • Penguin Group (NZ),
67 Apollo Drive, Rosedale, North Shore 0632, New Zealand (a division of Pearson New Zealand Ltd) •
Penguin Books (South Africa) (Pty) Ltd, 24 Sturdee Avenue, Rosebank, Johannesburg 2196, South Africa

Penguin Books Ltd, Registered Offices:
80 Strand, London WC2R 0RL, England

Library of Congress Cataloging-in-Publication Data

Ross, Carne.
The leaderless revolution : how ordinary people will take power and change
politics in the twenty-first century / Carne Ross.
p.   cm.
ISBN 978-0-399-15872-8
1. Political sociology.   2. Social change—Political aspects.   3. Political participation.
4. Political culture.   I. Title.
JA76.R653   2011   2011047493
306.2—dc23

Printed in the United States of America
1   3   5   7   9   10   8   6   4   2

BOOK DESIGN BY MEIGHAN CAVANAUGH

TO I AND C

War will be dead, the scaffold will be dead, frontiers will be dead, royalty will be dead, dogmas will be dead, man will begin to live.

Victor Hugo

The revolution will not be televised.

Gil Scott-Heron

CONTENTS

PREFACE: GUIDE TO
THE LEADERLESS REVOLUTION

> Turning and turning in the widening gyre
> The falcon cannot hear the falconer;
> Things fall apart; the centre cannot hold;
> Mere anarchy is loosed upon the world,
> The blood-dimmed tide is loosed, and everywhere
> The ceremony of innocence is drowned;
> The best lack all conviction, while the worst
> Are full of passionate intensity.*

Things do not seem to be going as planned. The system is broken. Meant to bring order, it foments instead disorder. We need something new.

The end of the Cold War was supposed to presage the triumph of democracy and, with it, stability. Globalization was supposed to launch everyone upon an eternally rising wave of prosperity. Some called it "the end of history." But history has instead opened another, unpredicted, chapter.

---

*William Butler Yeats, "The Second Coming," 1921.

While the opening of markets in India and China has released hundreds of millions from poverty, globalization has also triggered violent and uncontrolled economic volatility. Trillions of dollars shift from asset to asset (or from debt to debt), sometimes faster than a human can press a computer key—for it is an algorithm that controls the trade. Banks and whole countries crash, almost without warning. Meanwhile, the gap between a tiny number of the very rich and everyone else has accelerated rapidly, in every region and in every country.

The profits of this modern economy flow to a minuscule minority that holds the wealth closely. All the rest—the middle class and the poor—have seen their incomes stagnate over the last decade or so. And stagnation in reality means decline, as food and energy prices, driven by rising shortage, have risen faster and faster. And for those in the bottom 10 percent, incomes have declined in absolute, as well as relative, terms. Though they live cheek by jowl with the rich and share the same cities, the poor are getting poorer. In New York City, one in five children is dependent on food stamps for survival.

In every profession and trade, global competition means that jobs and careers once thought of as safe are no longer. Industries that have stood for generations can collapse in a few years. Few people now can look forward to a secure retirement.

The promise of capitalism seems more and more hollow. As its benefits are ever more unevenly shared, it has created a culture that cherishes much that is worst in human nature. Too much modern work is demeaning or humiliating, or simply boring. Little offers meaning.

In the exhausting yet often banal race to get ahead or at least to make ends meet, there is little time for others, for the community that seems ever more fractured, or for an ever more poisoned planet. Nature is no more, there is only what we have made of it. As *The Economist* recently put it, we live in the Anthropocene era: an Earth formed primarily by man.

Despite the dismal familiarity of these problems, credible solutions are hard to come by. Celebrities launch simplistic "single issue" campaigns, absurdly claiming that an e-mail to a representative will solve the problem. Each new cohort of politicians offers to fix this malaise, but they are less and less believed by others, and, one suspects, themselves (for they too can sense the mounting unease). Indeed, the political class now appears more part of the problem than the solution. Even politicians complain about "politicians."

In Britain, politicians and media crow over the humbling of press baron Rupert Murdoch, but barely admit that both estates were grossly corrupted by him, and for decades. In Washington, needless political bickering has managed to worsen America's debt problem—and increase the cost paid, eventually, by all Americans. "Washington" has become synonymous with ugly partisan argument and deadlock.

In democratic systems, it has become evident what is more obvious in autocracies—power is monopolized by the powerful. In the U.S., corporate lobbyists far outnumber legislators (there are now lobbyists for the lobbying industry). Legislation is sometimes created simply for political parties to extract rents from corporate interests. Big business donates to all parties, careful to ensure that its interests are protected whichever prevails. For it is still money that wins elections, and it is still large corporations that contribute the most.

In the 2008 "credit crunch," irresponsible and untransparent lending by banks and inadequate legislation (loosened by well-funded lobbying of both U.S. parties) combined to wreak massive and lasting damage on the world economy, affecting the poorest most of all. But despite this disaster, there is little sign of effective rules, national as well as global, judged by impartial experts as effective.

Banks lobby country by country to water down regulation, arguing that national competitiveness will be undermined—even though all the biggest banks operate in many markets at once. And at the international level, as so often is the case, governments are unable to agree on anything but the lowest common denominator, and even then often fail to implement it—as is clear with the so-called Basel III rules, which are claimed to bring banks back under control. In another equally important forum, after years of elaborate multitracked negotiations involving thousands of delegates in hundreds of meetings, there remains little prospect of international agreement on the necessary measures to limit carbon emissions.

And of the mounting evidence of this fundamental ineffectiveness and indeed corruption, the most striking piece of all is that the wealthy pay less tax, proportionately, than the poor. Returns on investment, such as hedge funds, are taxed at a far lower rate than the income tax levied on ordinary wage earners. Striking too is that complaints about this gross inequity are almost never to be heard in our supposedly representative parliaments.

So what is to be done? Voting for someone different at the next election seems a pathetically inadequate response—and it is. In Manhattan's Zuccotti Park, where the Occupy Wall Street protests have been centered, few have demanded different politicians or new laws. Instead, the protesters have shown, by the nature of their movement, a new way: debates and decisions that include everyone, a culture of collaboration and sharing, and a belief that there are many changes, not one, necessary to make a better world. No one claims the right to lead this movement: There are many voices that want to be heard. But although Occupy Wall Street is a sharp cry of anger echoed by many across the U.S., and indeed more widely around the world, the protest alone will not be enough.

What is needed is a much more fundamental, wholly new *method* of doing things. No longer should we look for change to emerge from untrusted politicians, arguing in distant chambers. As turkeys will not vote for Thanksgiving or Christmas, these institutions will not reform themselves. We have to accept the painful reality that we can no longer rely on government policy to solve our most deep-seated and intractable problems, from climate change to social alienation. Instead, we need to look to ourselves for the necessary action.

THERE ARE FOUR SIMPLE IDEAS at the heart of *The Leaderless Revolution*. Together, they suggest a radically different approach to conducting our affairs.

The first is that in an increasingly interconnected system, such as the world emerging in the twenty-first century, the action of one individual or a small group can affect the whole system very rapidly. Imagine the world as a sports stadium, where a "wave" can be started by just one person, but quickly involves the whole crowd. Those most powerful are right beside us; and we—in turn—are best placed to influence them. A suicide bomber acts, assaults his enemy and recruits others all in one horrible action: a technique with such effect that it has spread from Sri Lanka to Lebanon, Iraq and Afghanistan, Bali, London and New York within a few short years. But the same lesson is taught, with greater force, by peaceful acts, a truth shown by Mahatma Gandhi as well as the heroic young women, some still unknown, who refused to move to the back of the bus in the 1950s and 1960s American South. Modern network theory shows how one action can rapidly trigger change throughout the whole system. One person becomes a group, then becomes a movement; one act believed in and repeated by others becomes material, dramatic change.

The second key idea is that it is action that convinces, not words. New research is now demonstrating what good theater directors have always known: *Show,* don't tell. The actions of those people closest to us—and not government policy or even expert opinion—are the most influential. This means that Internet petitions are not likely to bring about fundamental change, although they might make the signatory feel better (which may indeed be the purpose). Likewise, social media may help organize and inform larger groups in ways that have never been available before, but unless this organization is used for a purpose—to *do* something—it is worthless.

In contrast to asking for or voting for someone else to do it, action can address the problem directly. There is an education intrinsic to action—you have to learn about the problem to solve it, for most problems are complex. This education reverses the infantilization and ignorance that authority encourages: *You* need not worry about the details, because *we* will take care of it. Equally, it demolishes the common notion that ordinary people are somehow incapable of making intelligent decisions about their own circumstances. Again, evidence shows this to be an arrogant fallacy—people know their own circumstances best of all.

The third key idea is about engagement and discussion. Again it is a simple idea: Decision making is better when it includes the people most affected. In the current Western model of representative democracy, we have become accustomed to the idea that politicians, elected by us, should negotiate among competing interests and make the necessary compromises to produce consensus and policy. In Washington today, it is painfully clear that this is the opposite of what is actually happening, while in Europe political consensus around the social democratic model is breaking down. The far right is emerging once more as a significant political force, in reaction to the largely unpredicted and sometimes violent changes that the world is now experiencing. In times of uncertainty, the false appeal of those who loudly proclaim certainty gains luster.

In Brazil, Britain and New Orleans, a better way of deciding our affairs together is emerging (and it is *not* the Internet, or *on* the Internet). It resembles democracy in its earliest and purest days—people gathering together, not in chat rooms, to make real decisions for themselves, not voting for others to decide on their behalf, or merely ventilate their frustrated opinions in town hall meetings or on the World Wide Web. When lobbyists fill what used to be called the people's parliaments and congresses, this alternative "participatory" democracy offers something unfamiliar yet extraordinary.

When large numbers of people make decisions for themselves, the results are remarkable: Everyone's views are heard, policies take all interests into account (as all lasting policy must), and are thus fairer. Facts and science are respected over opinion. Decision making becomes transparent (and thus less corrupt), respectful and less partisan—people who participate in decisions tend to stick to them. More responsibility and trust in society can come about only by giving real decision-making responsibility to people. If you do not give people responsibility, they tend to behave irresponsibly, and sometimes violently. Happily, the converse is also true: Give people power and responsibility, and they tend to use it more wisely—and peacefully.

This hints at the fourth idea that suffuses the argument throughout *The Leaderless Revolution*: agency—the power to decide matters for ourselves. We have lost agency. We need to take it back. We have become too detached from the decisions most important to us; we are disconnected, alienated, including from one another. This has contributed to a deeper ennui about modern life: What is it all for? Where is the meaning? What is the point? And in the solution to this crisis, which is both personal and political, something profound may be available.

If we take back agency, and bring ourselves closer to managing our affairs for ourselves, then something else may also come about: We may find a fulfillment and satisfaction, and perhaps even a meaning, which so often seems elusive in the contemporary circumstance.

These four ideas form the core of the philosophy of *The Leaderless Revolution*. Adopt these ideas, above all act upon them, and things will change. The book is intended as a guide and not a prescription. It sets out a *method* of doing things and taking action, and not what the outcome of this method should be. That is for everyone—acting together—to determine, and no single individual can pretend to know it, let alone a writer tapping away on a laptop. No one can claim to know what others truly want. These needs and concerns—and dreams—can be expressed only through action, shared decision-making and discussion with those most affected, including those who might disagree. But this method is the essence of a new form of politics, indeed a new way of living together on our crowded planet.

How might these ideas play out in practice? While the aspirations of this philosophy are grand, the steps needed to embody it are simple: small steps, things that everyone can do, every day.

It is no small struggle merely to live out the ideals that you aspire to. The first step, and perhaps the most important, is to work out what your ideals are. The slogan "Be the change you wish to see" is often associated with the environmental movement, but it applies more universally. At the simplest level, you cannot expect a political goal of "equality" if you treat people unequally or tolerate that treatment for others. People are not mere factors of production (or "utility-maximizing consumers"), as economists would depict them. By altering our conduct and thus our impact, we may incite change in others far away, with surprising force and speed.

One essential of any method of change is this: Consult those most affected. Those suffering from the problem (which may include you) will know far more about its dimensions and likely solutions. People will reject strident argument; they rarely reject informed interest. When I served as a diplomat, I was subjected to both. The reader will already know which had the more effect.

And it's important, in all this, to reject the easy sanctimony of the so-called Golden Rule: It exhibits a profound solipsism, if not arrogance, that we can know the requirements of others. Instead, the maxim should be to *ask* others what they want, and not assume. They always know, and now, thanks to the Internet, we can hear their voices, all over the world, with more clarity and vigor than ever before. If in any doubt, addressing those in most suffering is a good place to start, as Karl Popper once suggested, for unlike "happiness," suffering is all too easy to recognize and measure.

So much for the personal; now, how to change the workplace?

Here, the dominant model is the private company whose primary and overriding purpose is to maximize profit. The volatile flow of "hot money" from poor to well-performing stocks in the stock market, usually based on very short-term actual or predicted returns, reinforces this tendency. Meanwhile, a culture has arisen where bosses pay themselves hundreds of times more than what their average employees earn, sometimes regardless of performance. And government ownership has been proven a disastrously inefficient alternative. But there is another way to run a business, less often mentioned.

Consider cooperative companies, like Britain's retail chain John Lewis, that share ownership, as well as agency, in the company. All partners (not "employees") share in the profits and, notably, in decisions about the company's future. Differences in pay between the bosses and the others are far lower. Yet this company, for example, has been an enduring success, profiting and growing year after year in the most ferocious of markets. It has lasted nearly a century.

Such enterprises are not created by government legislation, or by the inevitable machinations of the market. They are established by the free choice of their owners and founders—people who choose to follow and propagate a different way of doing things, without abandoning the entrepreneurship that drives innovation and growth. And by their very nature, and embodiment of values other than mere profit seeking, these companies produce benefits that are today rarely associated with the modern company: equality, solidarity and a satisfaction of real involvement—as well as sustained economic stability. Contrast this with the feelings most wage slaves associate with their employers. Typically, one New York store owner told me that his biggest management problem was to create a sense of "ownership" in his business. But it is absurd to hope for "ownership" among employees who do not own any part of the business.

Then there are the banks. The current system drives banks to lend recklessly in boom times as they are forced to compete for profit and share price, or else face buy-out. A more robust system might consist of depositor-owned banks offering mutualized loans, where risk is spread transparently.* There is no intrinsic reason why such a bank should not be set up—indeed, there are already such—but it takes a decision by a brave group to take the first step, and decisions by depositors to reward institutions driven by values other than pure profit. This is a politics of personal action: at home, with one another, and in the workplace, incorporating the political goals we desire into everything we do.

In turn, consumers can reward these companies with their dollars. There are websites that offer competitive alternatives to the products of companies that exploit their workers or the environment. At the most extreme, customers can organize a boycott of the most egregious offenders, as depositors at one European bank did to protest the bonuses paid to executives after a huge government bailout (the bonuses were withdrawn and the government outlawed them for all bailed-out banks). When you're buying, you're voting. Every act becomes political. Indeed, it always was.

This simple method of action applies at the global level too. The Internet is now witnessing the genesis of online *movements*, where people sharing a common concern unite across borders to address it, not through campaigns but through action. We all know intuitively it simply isn't enough to fight genocide in Darfur or sex trafficking by clicking a button.

In the 1930s, forty thousand foreign volunteers traveled to Spain to fight fascism. Ten thousand never returned. These were extreme circumstances but illustrate the debilitating late-twentieth-century decline from acting to campaigning, a shift that has entirely suited

---

*A crucial factor behind the crisis wrought by the selling of "credit default options" (or "credit default swaps") in the 2008 financial crisis was that these products, initially designed to *spread* risk, in actual practice obscured it, because purchasers of the CDOs did not properly understand the risk they entailed.

the powerful. It is now abundantly clear, as it ever was, that it is action that makes a difference. If concerned about refugees from a distant war, give refuge. Boycott the aggressor's corporate partners. Build systems of cooperation and action, so it is no longer necessary to rely on the cumbersome reaction of our governments, which, as I have seen as a diplomat, too often act upon an artificial calculus of "national interests" that relegate human needs beneath those of the state or commerce.

No one pretends that it is easy to set up these alternative systems, but neither is it impossible. Like a modern-day version of Voltaire's Pangloss, who endlessly repeated that "all is for the best in the best of all possible worlds," it is tediously restated that the current status quo is immutable and, certainly, incapable of improvement. We are encouraged to believe that no one has the power to change it. Thus paralyzed, we are frozen into inaction. This paralysis of thought is the greatest obstacle to overcome. Defeat it, and everything becomes possible.

THE LEADERLESS REVOLUTION is not demanding the violent overthrow of government, or anything else. Everything worth changing can be changed without resorting to violence; this should be a gentle revolution, using force more lasting and convincing than any violence—our own actions and convictions. The most extreme cases of savage repression or attack may justify violence, and then only rarely, and only after all nonlethal alternatives including isolation, boycott and sabotage have been exhausted.

The Leaderless Revolution instead advocates the construction of an alternative and better system, step by small step.

Power must be taken back to where it rightfully belongs—to those who have, until now, let it be given away. No government will decree this. No politician will declare his own irrelevance. But we do not need orders from authority to take control. It can succeed at the simplest level, as well as on a broader canvas.

Self-organization need not and should not be an antagonistic process. Simply start talking to your neighbors. Identify shared concerns, and take action. Establish forums to discuss common issues, moderate these respectfully and inclusively, invite all those concerned to attend—and to speak.

In this way, these new forms of organization will gain legitimacy, a legitimacy of real popular consent, delivered through participation. Soon politicians will start to refer to these new forums, then bow to them, and one day perhaps give way to them. An alternative system is created.

At work, the same thing is possible. Unions once performed this organizing purpose, and still can, if they are truly inclusive and democratic—and not outlawed. But it can happen informally too. It can start with a few people meeting weekly over coffee, but as it builds and others join, those in charge will have to take notice. True power comes not from the assertion of rules and threats, but from the aggregation of honest and sincere voices, and their concerted heartfelt action. When sustained, uncorrupted and driven by real concerns, such power is ultimately irresistible. Thus is power taken back.

The Leaderless Revolution challenges the stale choice between free markets and government control. There is a better way that celebrates and releases the power of individual passion and enterprise, yet also expresses that equally deep-seated but less celebrated human trait: concern for others, responsibility for the common good and a belief that the most important things in life—community, love, purpose, one another—cannot be bought, but have to be enacted, striven for, *lived.*

But before any of this, the fear must be overcome—fear of one another, fear of ridicule or failure and, perhaps most inadmissible of all, fear of our own considerable power, as yet unleashed. It is this fear that authority plays upon, indeed relies upon: Only *we* can protect you. But that claim is ever less plausible in the face of global forces that are, increasingly, out of control, whether terrorism, climate change or economic volatility. Indeed, governments' attempts to impose order, through force or legislation, not only seem ineffective but may exacerbate the problems they are claimed to solve. Worse, they have convinced us, who have in fact the greater power, that we are powerless.

We have been silenced by the pervasive belief that there is no better system than the current one of profit-driven capitalism and representative democracy, when in fact our democracy has been hijacked by those with the largest profits. We have been intimidated by the bullying repetition that the status quo represents the summit of human progress to date, when in its inequality, its carelessness for our planet and its inhumanity to our fellow humans, in many ways it represents the worst. Our silence permits this outrage to continue, and profound injustice to be perpetuated. And it is this silence that must now be broken, through a thousand acts of construction to build a better world, a thousand acts that declare that there is a much, much better way of organizing and deciding our lives together. Though peaceful, these are revolutionary acts.

And with those acts, a new vista may open up, a possibility for the human endeavor far more exciting and inspiring than that offered by the current way of thought. Economic progress is not the measure of who we are, just as bickering politicians should not define our ability for cooperation. We are far more than merely this. And this possibility cannot be defined; it can only be enacted. This revolution can only succeed, indeed can only begin, without leaders: led by us—*in control*, at last.

Carne Ross
New York City
October 2011

INTRODUCTION:
THE SHEER CLIFF FACE

Some stories from the young twenty-first century:

When the H1N1 "swine flu" virus struck Mexico in early 2009, it took only hours and days to spread to every continent in the world except unpopulated Antarctica. Authorities struggled to contain the spread of the disease. Desperate to prevent the import of infection, some governments resorted to aiming remote thermometers at arriving air passengers to measure their body temperature. The World Health Organization, responsible for global coordination of the fight against disease, admitted some months after the first outbreak that it had been unable to keep up with the vast flow of data from national health bodies. The virus, it later appeared, was spreading out of control.

One Sunday that same year, a preacher from a Sikh sect was attacked during a service in Vienna, Austria. Sant Ramanand was set upon by six men armed with knives and a pistol and died early the next day. Within a few hours, widespread riots had broken out across the Punjab, where the preacher's sect was based. By nightfall—some six hours after Sant Ramanand had died—several people had been killed in turmoil that had convulsed Punjabi towns and cities. Thousands of Sikhs took to the streets, clashing with police and setting fire to buildings and vehicles. Major highways were blocked by bonfires of tires and sticks. Trains were attacked in several places. The authorities had little or no warning of the outbreak.

One afternoon in 2010, it took less than thirty minutes for the Dow Jones Industrial Average to fall nearly a thousand points—the biggest one-day points decline in the Dow's history. It took five months for regulators to explain what happened. According to the Securities and Exchange Commission report, the rapid plunge was triggered by a poorly executed sale by one mutual fund company. The firm started to sell $4.1 billion of futures contracts through an algorithmic trade, mistakenly taking account of only volume, not time or price. Buyers, including "high-frequency" traders who make rapid high-volume purchases and sales to exploit tiny price margins in a dynamic market, purchased the contracts. As sales of the contracts accelerated, the seller's algorithm responded to the increase in volume by unloading the contracts faster, pushing prices down further. The liquidity crunch then spread to the equity market. Many traders withdrew from the market. Some reverted to manual systems but could not keep up with the spike in volume. As the market dived, shares in some household-name companies were sold for as little as a cent. The SEC's report was widely criticized for offering no effective prescription on how to prevent such disruption in future.[1]

In the summer of 2008, food prices increased dramatically across the globe thanks, it seems, to a sudden surge in oil prices, although the causes of the spike are not fully understood. One factor may have been the introduction of subsidies for ethanol production in the U.S. Congress. Another possibility, speculation. The rocketing prices caused riots and political tension in Cairo and Indonesia and many other countries and reinforced an already emerging trend that some have called a "food crunch" of static global supply and rising demand.[2] The prices of commodities such as rice and wheat jumped to record highs, triggering food riots from Haiti to Egypt to Bangladesh and Cameroon and prompting UN appeals for food aid for more than thirty countries in sub-Saharan Africa.

In response to this phenomenon, companies and in some cases governments in money-rich but "food-poor" countries, like South Korea and Saudi Arabia, began to buy up land and agricultural rights in money-poor but land-rich countries. The Saudi Star company plans to spend up to $2 billion in the next few years acquiring and developing 500,000 hectares of land in Ethiopia, one of the poorest—and hungriest—in the world.[3] Up to fifty million hectares of land—an area more than double the size of Britain—has been bought in the last few years or is under negotiation by governments and wealthy investors, often enjoying state subsidies. The South Korean company Daewoo bought the rights to as much as half of Madagascar's available agricultural land. This deal in turn helped trigger a coup against the Malagasy government that signed the deal. This coup produced political instability in Madagascar that continues to the time of this writing.

Earlier in the century, an Egyptian architecture student living in Hamburg was horrified by reports of Russia's brutal campaign against separatists, mostly Muslim, in Chechnya in the Southern Caucasus, a war whose atrocities were scarcely reported in the information-overloaded citadels of the West. The Chechnya war confirmed his view of the global oppression of Muslims. Mohamed Atta joined a local mosque where, it was later learned, he was introduced to the concept of jihad, a personal struggle for liberation.

Atta made his way to Pakistan, to join a terrorist network called Al Qaeda, or "The Base," which had been founded—and funded—by a middle-aged man who himself had been radicalized by the Soviet Union's occupation of Muslim Afghanistan—as well as America's military domination of his home country, Saudi Arabia. In the Afghan mujahideen victory over the Soviet occupation forces, Osama bin Laden found his inspiration to seek a global jihad. Mohamed Atta was to become the pilot of the American Airlines Boeing 767 which cannoned into the north tower of New York's World Trade Center. Walking to work that dread morning, I heard his aircraft fly overhead.

The singular act of the 9/11 attacks helped trigger the allied invasions of two countries, and further massive, complex and unforeseeable change. The attacks were brilliantly anatomized in the U.S. Congress *9/11 Commission Report*, which took over eight hundred pages to describe the antecedents and chronology of this one single, if remarkable, event—and *that* was concise.

More recently, the defaults of a few subprime mortgage holders concentrated in just three American states triggered in a very short space of time a global economic meltdown that—among many, many other things—brought down several long-established banks in the United States and necessitated a $700 billion bailout of other banks. When confidence in the ability of U.S. banks to meet their obligations collapsed, rapid contraction of credit was contagious across the globe, destroying in quick time both overleveraged banks, and the deposits of their customers. Banks in Iceland fell overnight, eliminating at a stroke the savings of depositors in the UK. The ramifications of that event continue to delay Iceland's entry into the European

Union, while in Britain the credit crunch, among other factors, has contributed to the most severe austerity measures and government spending cuts in many decades, including a 70 percent cut to higher education budgets. In Hong Kong, thousands of small investors and pensioners suddenly lost their Lehman "mini-bonds," worth billions of dollars, when Lehman Brothers, founded in 1850, fell in the U.S.[4]

The origins of the "credit crunch" were manifold and are debated still. Greedy lending by banks, unwise borrowing by home buyers, loosening legislation from government, enacted with the worthy intention of enabling broader home ownership: perhaps all of them played a part. But some have suggested a more deep-seated cause—the growing inequality in America between the rich and everyone else, which drove the income-stagnant middle classes to borrow ever more to maintain their living standards amid rising costs.

Another intriguing factor has been barely noted. The statistical models used by the banks to assess the risks of bundled mortgages were out of date: Not only did they underestimate the volume and riskiness of the increasingly popular subprime mortgages, the banks' models also underestimated interconnectedness within the housing and mortgage markets, regionally and nationally. The preponderance of the "no money down" high debt-to-deposit subprime mortgages meant that only a small dip in the economy made huge numbers of mortgages suddenly unaffordable, and the buyers defaulted. The banks had underestimated the degree to which one thing would lead quickly to many others. They underestimated complexity.

Whatever the cause, no government was ready for the crash, which came almost without warning. Then President George W. Bush said later that he had been "blindsided" by the crisis, stating that he "assumed any major credit troubles would have been flagged by the regulators or credit agencies."[5] The cascading and multiple effects of the "credit crunch," many of which have yet to be felt, included the loss of tens of millions of jobs around the globe, and an immeasurable but nonetheless notable shift of power from West to East, as the U.S. relied ever more heavily upon China to buy up almost a trillion dollars' worth of American government debt to finance the government bailout.

THE TORTURED, TWISTING PATHS from cause to effect in these stories of the twenty-first century are discernible only in retrospect by separating out these threads from the confusing rats' nest of simultaneous events—itself a somewhat artificial and falsifying exercise. But these stories are not extraordinary. They are typical of a vastly interconnected age, when billions and billions of people are interacting constantly, a wholly unprecedented phenomenon that we are only beginning to understand. These events were not predictable by most conventional theories of politics or economics.

Some may see chaos in these events, or purely random cause and effect. These events do not suggest the structured order of past experience—of units, be they states or individuals, behaving according to established theories of international relations or neoclassical economics, predictable for the most part, and comprehensible within our existing models. But neither are they chaos, a random, meaningless mess. They are something else. This is a new dispensation—complexity—requiring new tools: the science of complex systems. Pioneers in many fields are using techniques like agent-based modeling and network analysis to begin to offer powerful new insights into this multiplying complexity.

But this new world requires something else beyond new tools of interpretation. This world is defying the ability of existing structures and institutions to understand and arbitrate events effectively. Even senior government officials confess the decline of state power: "We are in a world where governments, as a whole, have less power than they once did," a senior U.S. State Department official recently said, sensibly concluding, "Let's take the world as we now see it."[6] Confidential briefing papers prepared for the UN Secretary-General noted the declining importance not only of the UN itself, but also of governments in managing the world's most pressing political, economic and environmental problems, observing cheerily that "Our planet's ability to sustain life, as we know it, is under enormous strain."[7] As Parag Khanna has commented:

> Globalization is . . . diffusing power away from the west in particular, but also from states and towards cities, companies, religious groups, humanitarian non-governmental organizations and super-empowered individuals, from terrorists to philanthropists. This force of entropy will not be reversed for decades—if not for centuries.[8]

Timothy Garton Ash has called this world "not a new world order but a new world disorder. An unstable kaleidoscope world—fractured, overheated, germinating future conflicts."[9] Governments failed to predict the credit crunch, as they did 9/11. Their blunt methods to manage both economic volatility and terrorism—as well as other global problems—are insufficient, and sometimes counterproductive.

Politicians argue that only if *they* are in power will decisions be the right ones, and thus we must suffer tedious rounds of facile political argument over enduring and deep-seated problems, when closer analysis of these problems leads to the more disturbing conclusion that no politician and no government, however wise, however right, is able to solve them. Somehow we know this. Frustration with conventional politics is rising everywhere, depressing voter turnout and fueling popular anger. Politicians too can sense the mood, but are unable to offer any prescription except more of the same politics, perhaps spiced with a dangerous and hollow populism.

This new world requires something else beyond more promises, something beyond new theories of interpretation, something that might, just might, make us at last feel that the tools might fit the job. This new world requires a new politics.

CLIMATE CHANGE, terrorism, ceaseless wars in places that defy understanding or resolution and where victory and defeat both seem far away,* a perpetual economic volatility—these are now already familiar problems of this young and turbulent century. They are easy problems to define: borderless, a product of the new "globalized" world. But at the same time they seem intractable: There seems very little that any individual can do about them.

Taking their allotted role, governments, and associations of governments—the UN, the EU, international conferences in Copenhagen or Doha—instead claim that *they* have these problems in hand. Every day witnesses a summit, a statement or a resolution claiming to address these worrying ills. It is a never-ending video feed of activity, tedious to watch in detail, but nonetheless reassuring in its unceasing activity and torrent of verbiage—at least, that is the intention.

"Trust us," the statements say, "we have these problems under

---

*The head of the British armed services, Sir David Richards, told the BBC in November 2010 that Al Qaeda could be only "contained" not defeated, saying that one cannot defeat "an idea." "West Cannot Defeat al-Qaeda, Says UK Forces Chief," BBC website, November 14, 2010. http://www.bbc.co.uk/news/world-middle-east-11751888.

control." But the evidence suggests otherwise, more and more insistently. Measure the *outputs*, not the promises made. Take two familiar problems.

At the 2009 Copenhagen climate change summit, an intensive two-year international negotiation involving hundreds of delegates from almost every country, and thousands of pressure groups and lobbyists, produced at its end a short two-page document which, in hastily drafted and ungrammatical prose, offers only the most general statements of concern about the problem of climate change and no binding commitments to limit carbon emissions or to compensate those most affected by its manifold impacts.

Despite the global membership of the negotiation, encompassing every country in the world, the statement was hashed out in the last few hours of the conference in a closed-room session involving China, Brazil, the U.S. and India. The needs of those most affected by climate change, like Bangladesh or low-lying island states that are already losing land to rising seas, were ignored.

The Copenhagen process had been formidably complicated, involving multiple "tracks" of negotiation in an attempt to address the many different aspects of the problem of climate change, including forests, technology transfer and protection of oceans as well as the "big picture" questions of carbon emissions and how to finance the costs of adapting to the effects of rising temperatures. Despite the thousands of hours spent negotiating these subsidiary issues over the previous two years, none of them was addressed in the final text.

In Cancún, a year later, delegates successfully agreed that their states wanted to limit global warming to 2°C—the "danger" level, beyond which, a recent paper in the scientific journal *Nature* warned, warming may increase beyond any control. The conference was widely touted as a "success," as the Mexican hosts managed to secure agreement on key issues, including financing for climate adaptation in poorer countries. But there was no agreement on how climate change might be prevented—concrete agreement on the carbon emissions targets that scientists concur as necessary. As *The Economist* reported, Cancún was successful in rescuing the UN climate negotiations "process"; its value in rescuing the climate was less clear.[10]

Recently, the UN Environment Programme reported that even if states fulfilled all of their commitments to reduce carbon emissions, including those made at Copenhagen, the world's temperature would still most likely exceed the 2°C danger level. Outside of predictions and commitments, and in the real world of the Earth's atmosphere, where success or failure is truly measured, the concentration of carbon in the atmosphere has continued to rise unabated. In 1992, at the time of the first international gathering of governments to address climate change,* the concentration of carbon in the atmosphere was 354 parts per million by volume. By 2010, it was nearly 10 percent higher, an unprecedentedly rapid increase.

Meanwhile, in the global economy, the years that immediately followed the 2008–2009 credit crunch witnessed innumerable G8, G20, UN and Basel Committee discussions attempting to agree on new standards and rules to prevent a recurrence of the devastating crash. But within the confusing barrage of statements and commitments on new task forces, committees and "watchdogs," nowhere to be found was the one simple measure—substantially higher capital/debt requirements for banks—that almost all disinterested analysts believe would actually prevent a crash happening again. And there was a reason for this absence.

---

*The so-called Earth Summit in Rio de Janeiro.

While globalization intensifies apace, its rigors and stresses ever more evident, its rewards seem to accrue mostly to a minority: The top 1 percent of the population in the U.S. took home nearly 25 percent of all income, the highest percentage since 1928.[11] Middle-class incomes are declining, but living expenses are not. Meanwhile, for many of the poorest, life has actually gotten worse.

Across the globe, more than one billion still live on less than one dollar per day; two billion live on a pathetic two dollars per day. And while it is easy to ignore the miseries of life in Somalia and Bangladesh, it is more astonishing that in New York City one in five children is dependent on food stamps for survival, while Goldman Sachs bankers enjoy bonuses of some $700,000 each and hedge fund traders throw parties costing hundreds of thousands. In 2011, as leading bankers declared that the "years of apology" should be over,[12] one study showed that seven million of the poorest Britons had seen their living standards decline by a massive 10 percent over the previous decade.[13] In 2009, one in seven Americans was living in poverty, the highest proportion of the population for fifty years. In some parts of America, life expectancy is actually declining thanks to poverty, though health care spending per capita—averaged across the population—is higher here than anywhere on earth.

As the whole world, except North Korea, adopts the capitalist model, such inequality is rising everywhere, both between and within countries. In China, the introduction of free market economics has freed hundreds of millions from poverty. But at the same time it has created the worst inequality in Asia, apart from Nepal, until very recently an autocratic monarchy: Official estimates suggest 1 percent of Chinese households enjoy 40 to 60 percent of total household wealth.[14] In India, politicians obsess about headline GDP growth rates, and the richest build billion-dollar skyscraper houses, but hundreds of millions remain in abject poverty and malnourishment—the calorie intake of the poorest has remained stagnant for over a decade, and more than half of India's children under five suffer stunting and poor brain development.[15] Even in the supposedly egalitarian Nordic countries, the gap between rich and poor is growing fast. Worldwide, a new trend has emerged, barely noticed: Beyond a certain level of development, those at the top benefit enormously, those at the bottom often actually do worse, while the income of the bulk of the population stays more or less stagnant.

It is little wonder, then, that this model is so confidently extolled as ideal by those who benefit from it. So often are the virtues of this system avowed that it has taken on the characteristics of a *moral* system, where anything done in the name of that system, however gross, is morally justified as part of the necessary mechanics of the market.

The future offers an unsettling vision of ever greater competition for markets and scarce resources. The ferocious contest of the global marketplace is like being chained to an accelerating treadmill, under constant pressure to cut costs and invent new products, trapped by a ceaseless desperation to attract customers who themselves are ever less satisfied, hopping from product to product (as surveys reveal), craving a satiation—a fulfillment—they can never find. As billions join the global labor force, no job is secure, no industry is stable, no profession may not one day face obsolescence.

While economic insecurity is on the rise, so too is a more insidious and equally permanent anxiety—political insecurity and violence. As U.S. officials with great candor admitted after 9/11, we are in a "Long War" with global terrorists, and it seems to be getting longer. The war with Al Qaeda is spreading across the world's geography, as its affiliates metastasize. The invasion of Afghanistan, whose rationale I delivered to the UN one winter morning,* wholly justified to remove the government brazenly hosting our attackers, not only has succeeded in perpetuating civil war in Afghanistan but also has triggered the spread of instability and extreme violence to the border areas and across Pakistan, where now every major city has seen repeated suicide attacks of horrific violence.

In the "homeland," violent jihadists may be found not just among immigrants and visitors, but in the ranks of our own population: "Jihad Jane," who was radicalized in her Philadelphia suburb; the U.S. Army doctor who killed thirteen and wounded thirty at Fort Hood. A third of all charged U.S. terror suspects are American citizens.[16] Contrary to the received wisdom that economic underdevelopment is the fount of terrorism, former CIA case officer Marc Sageman found in a study of 172 Al Qaeda terrorists that the majority were middle to upper class, well educated, married with children, and occupied professional or semi-professional positions, often as engineers, architects, scientists and doctors. In Britain, suicide attackers who killed fifty-six and injured several hundred on the London Underground and buses on July 7, 2005, came not from Saudi Arabia but from Dewsbury and Leeds. The would-be murderers who tried to detonate a nail bomb in a London nightclub in 2007 included a highly trained and British-born National Health Service doctor.

Thanks to the spread of technology—which can be as simple as cell phones and fertilizer—and information on the Internet, it is

---

*The letter set out the legal justification—self-defense—under Article 51 of the UN Charter for the United Kingdom's participation in the allied invasion.

now straightforward for small groups of extremists to kill large numbers of people. In Japan, police discovered that the Aum Shinrikyo sect had the capability to produce the deadly nerve gas sarin in aerosol form. Had they chosen to use this method, the fanatical group could have killed many hundreds. Instead, they chose to deploy the less toxic liquid form of the agent, but still killed scores and horribly injured many more.

In Oklahoma, Terry Nichols and Timothy McVeigh killed five hundred and injured thousands with a truck bomb assembled at a cost of less than $5,000. After mounting attempted attacks in 2010 to detonate package bombs on several airliners, the Yemeni branch of Al Qaeda (AQAP) announced "Operation Hemorrhage," part of a new approach eschewing major attacks, instead setting out to cause "death by a thousand cuts." "To bring down America we do not need to strike big," AQAP stated; the total bill for the parcel bomb operation was a mere $4,200, but it "will without a doubt cost America and other Western countries billions of dollars in new security measures. This is what we call leverage."[17]

Some 700,000 to 800,000 light weapons are produced every year, adding to the vast stock of weapons already in circulation, as many weapons remain in use decades after their manufacture—Taliban fighters carry AK-47s produced in the 1960s or earlier.[18] Countries like Austria, Canada, the UK and U.S. join North Korea, China and Russia as the largest producers of these weapons, the primary means of conflict worldwide. The annual authorized trade in such weapons exceeds $6 billion a year.[19] The *Small Arms Survey* now reckons that globally there are nearly 900 million light weapons, some of ever greater sophistication: sniper rifles deadly at a two-mile range; man-portable missiles that can down airliners; mines that can sink cruise liners. In Mexico, drug traffickers have used submarines and antitank missiles in their wars with one another and the authorities.

But it is not only the growing ubiquity of weapons and terrorism—what's in the backpack of that man down the railroad car?—that threatens our sense of safety and well-being. In Britain, the millions of CCTV cameras broadcast their own message of our lack of trust in one another. Some cameras now bear loudspeakers to broadcast their correctional message to the "antisocial." In some city centers, authorities deploy noise-making devices whose deterrent screech can be heard only by the young, like dogs or rats already designated as "troublemakers." Police are beginning to deploy unmanned drones with high-resolution cameras to monitor car traffic and the population, as defense companies push for military technology to be adopted in policing. Some of the drones carry loudspeakers with which to relay instructions to the civilian populace.[20] It is reported that the London 2012 Olympics will be monitored by Royal Air Force "Reaper" unmanned combat air vehicles (UCAVs), hitherto deployed in Afghanistan to attack insurgents.

Meanwhile, in the United States, nearly four thousand federal, state and local counterterrorism agencies monitor the population, while thirty thousand officials are employed solely to monitor telephone and other communications, creating, in the words of *The Washington Post*, "a new level of government scrutiny" of its citizens. Thousands of Americans are included in a vast database, including many who have never been accused of any wrongdoing.[21]

But the intrusiveness of such measures does little to lessen the evident tension in public spaces, nor deter random, almost casual violence. In 2008, Kevin Tripp had an argument with a stranger in a supermarket checkout queue in South London. The argument escalated. Tripp was punched to the ground, suffering serious head injuries. He died later in the hospital. In Baltimore in 2010, one man killed another with a chunk of concrete during an argument over a parking space.

Research data show that community life in Britain, and America, is deteriorating. Measuring the number of people in an area who are single, those who live alone, the numbers in private rented accommodation and those resident for less than a year, researchers found that all communities in Britain were "less rooted" than they were thirty years earlier.[22] Comparing data from a census taken in 1971, researchers at the University of Sheffield found substantially higher levels of "rootlessness" and "anomie" in contemporary communities. Commenting on this data, the research leader, Professor Daniel Dorling, said, "Even the weakest communities in 1971 were stronger than any community now." Ninety-seven percent of communities studied had become more fragmented over the last three decades. "These trends may be linked to higher likelihoods of fearfulness because we are less likely to see and therefore understand each others' lives."

In the U.S., over a similar period, the rate at which Americans invite people to their homes has declined by 45 percent. In his classic study *Bowling Alone*, Robert Putnam reported indices of discohesion and social fragmentation rising across the board. For instance, membership of chapter-based organizations, where members attend regular meetings and participate in social activities like the Rotary Club, the Masons, the NAACP, Boy and Girl Scouts, etc., halved in the last fifty years. Others report that Americans are also—unsurprisingly—lonelier. Between 1985 and 2004, the number of Americans who said they had no close confidants tripled. Single-parent households are on the rise, and the 2010 U.S. Census found that more than 31 million Americans live alone, over 30 percent more than in 1980.[23]

As if these data were not dismal enough, it seems too that the very ground on which we stand is less firm than before. Mankind foolishly believed that nature, once conquered, would remain quiescent in our plans. Rising sea levels have already required the evacuation—forever—of several low-lying islands. In Australia, forest fires rage with a new and terrifying ferocity, consuming whole towns. Even the skeptical notice greater volatility in the weather—everything's hotter and colder, and wetter and windier—than it used to be. This too is consistent with science's predictions. This volatility feeds a deeper disconnection between man and his environment. For the first time ever, more people now dwell in cities than the countryside. The urban majority now barely encounter what their forebears took for granted: trees, fresh air, birdsong, *silence*. Lives are lived out in a frantic, noisy hecticness; fulfillment is distant, with peace and escape dreamed of, sometimes purchased, but all too rarely experienced.

This list is so depressing that together these problems offer a sheer and intimidating cliff face, upon which there appears no handhold, no purchase at all. The temptation is simply to switch off, tune out, escape.

And indeed advertising offers us a tantalizing vision of that escape, a ceaseless promise to leave the burdensome everyday and wander into sunlit uplands: "Go forth!" says one advert for jeans, with an evocative image of a young man shirtless in a field of waving grass. These messages claim not only to sell us jeans but to solve our all-too-obvious, if never-to-be-admitted, existential crisis: That all this—the modern condition of prosperity, a sort of peace, a sort of freedom—is simply not enough. The yearning for more, for distraction, never quite goes away however much is purchased, however many holidays are taken.

This hunger is all but explicit in the advertising (Go forth! Find yourself! Choose freedom!), but can never be confessed in a culture where our arguments—capitalism, democracy—are supposed to have won, and provide a convincing, empirically justified answer to all objections, except the one we cannot admit to.

But in this existential crisis, the first fragile handhold upon the cliff face of intractable problems is revealed. The answer to both crises is, in fact, the same. And it is simple. It is embodied in one word: agency. Agency over events—the feeling of control—is a gross absence in the contemporary condition. Recapturing it is available through one simple mechanism: action. Action to reassert control over events in our lives. And this in a nutshell is the simple essence of the philosophy to be offered here. We lack control; we need to take it back.

THE INCREDIBLE AND SEISMIC changes of the late twentieth and early twenty-first centuries have forced dramatic and sometimes revolutionary changes in almost every realm of human activity—finance, technology, culture—but not in politics. In this most crucial forum, the institutions and habits acquired in different times have endured, even when their effectiveness is less and less evident. On the contrary, the evidence is accumulating that these inherited bodies and rules are less and less able to comprehend and arbitrate the forces now swirling around us.

Something else is desperately needed. That necessity has been articulated by many but none has offered a solution except more of the same, politics as usual: pathetic calls for more "political will" to address this or that problem; celebrity-endorsed "single issue" campaigns for the public to pressure their representatives to address one particular crisis over others; superficial online campaigns to address some deep and poisonous malaise, like starvation or child slavery. Some believe that technology alone will deliver the necessary revolution, but here too it is clear that technology's effects are often as malign as benign, serving the dictatorial as much as the democratic. A more fundamental shift is needed.

One telltale sign is the increasing number of politicians who now promise to "change politics" itself. In 2008, it was Barack Obama; in Britain, it was the Conservative/Liberal Democrat coalition of 2010 which promised to change the very nature of the system. In America, the change-the-system sentiment is now expressed by the Tea Party movement, with its demand to "take back our government." And just as surely, the Labour Party in Britain, now in opposition after thirteen years in government, will develop a new claim, that it too will "change the system" if only voters give them a chance. The pattern is a clear one. Politicians can smell the frustration, and must respond to it, but are surely doomed. With each electoral cycle, the disillusionment appears greater, data show that voters chop and change parties with greater frequency, while turnout falls steadily in all democracies, with only the occasional upward "blip," like the sputtering of a dying fire.

This revolution is as profound as it is simple. Evidence and research are now suggesting that the most important agent of change is ourselves. At a stroke, the prevailing notion that the individual is impotent in the face of the world's complex and manifold problems is turned on its head. Instead, the individual is revealed as a powerful motor of change, offering the prospect of immense consequences for politics and the world, and, no less, for himself.

I ONCE BELIEVED in the capability and rightness of enlightened government so fervently that I went to work for it. I was a British diplomat, in an institution and a system founded on a deep belief that state officials like me could understand and arbitrate the world effectively, for the benefit of the less informed masses. I no longer believe this. This disillusionment came not from ideological conversion, but from experience.

In my work on many of the world's most worrying problems, including climate change, terrorism and the wars in Afghanistan and Iraq (I was responsible for both issues for the UK at the United Nations), it became slowly clear to me that government was unable, by its very nature, to comprehend and manage these forces effectively. Why will become clear, but in short I realized, dimly and slowly, a profound and intrinsic deficit of governments: that they are required to take what is complex—reality—and turn it into simplistic pronouncements and policy, the better to convince the population that government has matters in hand. People in government are not bad or stupid, on the contrary; but the contract between people and government forces them to claim something which no sensible person should claim, that government—anyone!—can understand and predict the massive complexity of the contemporary world, and manage it on our behalf. Every politician must claim to the voters that they can interpret the world, and produce certain effects, just as the officials working for them must pretend that they can too. I know this because I did it.

I saw how in looking at places like the Middle East, and by extension the whole world, governments were forced to reduce hugely complicated and dynamic situations into simplistic models, us and them, security versus threat, just as they were required to project the manifold needs of their own diverse peoples into simple and artificially invented sets of "interests." Such a process is inherently false, requiring governments—and officials like me—to create stories and policies that offer clear, straightforward and therefore often very simplistic solutions. Then, to justify these stories, their officials must seek out the facts to suit the policy, the very opposite of a more valid empirical method—where we observe the world, then respond accordingly. Governments have it the wrong way around.

I gladly took part in such processes, writing speeches and talking points, and arguing in vicious negotiation to claim that Saddam's Iraq was a threat, that his regime's overthrow would deliver stability and spread democracy across the Middle East. On Afghanistan, I wrote embassy telegrams from a Kabul freshly liberated from the Taliban, explaining how democracy "Afghan style" would bring peace and prosperity to the Afghan people, conveniently overlooking the reality that much of Afghanistan remained unliberated from the Taliban's grip and that the democratic government we proclaimed was in fact largely our own creation, our own fantasy of what democracy *should* look like, rather than necessarily what the local people really wanted. After fifteen years as a diplomat, I was highly skilled in writing cables and reports and policy submissions that endlessly reaffirmed our version of events, often without the benefit of any knowledge from the ground at all. In five years working on Iraq, not once had I set foot in the country, yet at the UN, I was called Britain's Iraq "expert." I was not alone in such ignorance, nor in the arrogance that, despite it, government could declare with confidence what was happening or what might happen in such places. Only after much subsequent slow and sometimes painful reflection did I come to these broader conclusions about the intrinsic amorality, but also incapability, of government.

I watched dramatic forces at play in the world, and felt rising frustration at the seeming inability of government, or indeed anyone, to offer meaningful and plausible solutions. As political violence spread, and the credit crunch exploded, I watched desperate politicians, some of them friends, as they argued to pretend that they might understand, might control these forces—terrorism, the stresses of globalization, the deteriorating natural environment. I watched the growing angry chorus in public gatherings and on the Internet, demanding action, change, *something*, with ever more belligerent rhetoric, but never themselves offering solutions beyond a rejection of the current cohort of lousy politicians.

And I pondered change itself, how to react to this vastly complex world in a way that might work, that might provide the satisfaction of finding real traction upon the ghastly sheer cliff face of problems. And I realized that perhaps the worst deficit of government itself was this: In claiming to arbitrate the world's problems, unintentionally it encourages our own inaction and detachment. And in that detachment, rage and frustration has fermented dangerously. In the disembodied anonymity of the Internet, or the vapid chatter of commentators and newsreaders, and in the ceaseless demand for government and politicians to act—do something!—I saw how our opinions have become yet more polarized, an alienation from each other exacerbated by the mobility and rootlessness of modern economies. The problem is always someone else's, never ours, to solve.

And yet it is action—and only action—that changes things. Whether in the history of the battle for civil rights in America's South or the Franco-Russian wars, or in the contemporary research of social scientists and network theorists, the same ancient truth is repeated: It is the action of individuals that has the most effect on those around them, their circumstances, and thus the whole world. Whether in Gandhi's Salt March to free India from colonial rule, or in the efforts of a group of New York City men to stop muggings in their neighborhood, the expression of conviction through action has the most powerful impact on us and others, our surroundings, indeed our own well-being. The scale of the world's difficulties—the sheer cliff face—and the magnitude of globalization produce a paralyzing sense of impotence and frustration. But in fact, in a world that is more interconnected than ever before, with each person only a few links from anyone else, actions in our own microcosmos can have global consequences.

These stories and ideas will be explored in this book: facts, research and stories that together suggest a radical philosophy of how to create a better world, one that more closely reflects the current reality than the easy but dangerous assumption that we can leave it all to government to fix. This philosophy could fit under the broad school of thought known as "anarchism," a term commonly associated with violence and nihilism—more what it is against, than what it is for. And mere opposition to government, authority and hierarchy is clearly insufficient as a solution. This book has a more positive vision, presented in detailed principles to guide action. It is not proposing a violent overthrow of government, but a much gentler revolution—in the way we think about the world, and how we—ourselves—might therefore respond to it. Changing our own approach is critical: embodying our political beliefs in every action. Changing the self may change the world. In all the haze and chatter, rediscover what you truly believe in, then *act*. And following that transformation, another necessary shift—negotiating directly with one another, rather than leaving it to distant institutions. In contrast to the paralysis of modern legislatures, too often dominated by the interests of the powerful rather than the mass, collective decision making, whether in New Orleans or Brazil, has emphatically shown the benefits of shared debate and responsibility: respect for one another, for facts, and above all, agreement upon better, fairer and more enduring solutions.

In a world where government influence is in inexorable decline, and other transnational forces assert themselves, some beneficent but some malign, there is little choice but to take on the burden of action ourselves. If we do not, others surely will, whether criminal mafias with worldwide reach, global terrorist movements or multinational companies and banks with no concern but their own profit. This book offers some simple pointers to what that action might comprise—conviction, action, consultation—with some inspiring stories of how these principles have worked before. But this is no historical survey; it is an attempt to look at the world as it actually is, not as we or governments might wish it to be, and design a plan of action to respond. It is above all a manifesto about *how* to act—method—not a prescription of *what* end-state or utopian system to seek. No book can offer solutions to every problem, though there are several suggestions here. But that *how* is the key, for, as we shall see, the method is the point—the means are the ends. In that method, there are extraordinary prizes to be won—not only the accomplishment of the desired goal, but a greater sense of cooperation, respect and community with our fellow human beings, and a deeper sense of our own satisfaction and purpose, needs that are all but ignored in the current obsession with material well-being, status and celebrity. It is a humble and very practical manifesto, though its ideals are transcendent.

In the current crisis there are small but glimmering signals that point the way forward. These signals are but rarely noticed by those who defend the current order, but the lessons of this new philosophy are all around us, if we care to look. You won't find this teaching in the academy, or in economists' predictions or politicians' speeches.

1

THE WAVE AND
THE SUICIDE BOMBER

When American troops entered Iraq in 2003, they were briefed to expect a conventional army consisting, as such armies do, of tanks, artillery and infantry. Saddam Hussein's army had once contained more Main Battle Tanks, a primary unit of the conventional army, than all the armies of Western Europe put together.*

The lead elements of the American and British armies, then, were surprised to find that most of the opposition they faced was not tanks and howitzers, but men in pickup trucks, bearing rocket-propelled

---

*As an official working during the first Gulf War with Iraq in 1991, I had as one of my duties to count Saddam's tanks and soldiers in such a way as to affirm the claim, not strictly true but made by a politician and therefore requiring some kind of validation, that Iraq had "the third-largest army in the world." This claim could be "proven" only if all the reserve forces of the Iraqi army were included in the count, but if corresponding reserve forces were ignored in counting the armies of competitors for the third-place slot (India, the United States, Russia).

grenades (RPGs) and machine guns. These bands would attempt to ambush the advancing allied columns, launch the RPGs, then flee. They were not often successful. Indeed, so desperate and dangerous to their participants were these attacks that they resembled nothing so much as the Japanese kamikaze suicide attacks familiar from the Pacific theater of the Second World War. These *fedayeen* fighters, as they came to be known, did not appear to belong to particular Iraqi army units, or if they did, their members had abandoned the uniforms and badges that denoted their unit allegiance.

The allied invasion proceeded with remarkably little substantial opposition. The American tanks at the head of the advance reached Baghdad almost as fast as they could drive. The capital quickly fell, the statues of the hated dictator were toppled and the allies assumed control of the country, taking possession of the main government buildings abandoned by Saddam's cohorts and thus, they believed, control.

It was only in the days that followed that the real military opposition to the invasion began to assert itself. The first suicide attack had taken place during the march on Baghdad. The attacker—an Iraqi army officer dressed in civilian clothes—drove a taxi to a checkpoint near the central city of Najaf and, as American soldiers approached, detonated the vehicle. Four soldiers were killed.[1] Iraq's then vice president, Taha Ramadan, warned that there would be many more such "martyrdom missions": He was right, though the attacks that followed were not under government orders; his government would soon disappear. A few days later, two women suicide bombers killed three coalition soldiers north of Baghdad.

Over the days and months that followed, the number of suicide bombings rose dramatically. In one month in 2004, there were several attacks every day. As Dexter Filkins reported in *The New York*

Times, "In the first five years, more than nine hundred people detonated themselves in Iraq, sometimes several in a single day. That was
before you counted the car bombs when the driver got out before it
exploded. There were thousands of those."[2]

Suicide bombers used cars, trucks and motorbikes; often they
came on foot, sometimes on bicycles. During the "surge" of American troops in 2008, attackers launched fusillades of massive "lob
bombs"—explosive-filled gas cylinders propelled by crude rocket
engines—from flatbed trucks parked alongside U.S. bases. The operators, their intent clearly suicidal, were inevitably annihilated, but
only after unleashing hours of bombardment. Such were the ferocity
and effectiveness of the attacks, and the allies' inability effectively to
stop them, that they began to undermine the will of the U.S. to remain. Even before Barack Obama's election as president in 2008,
when during the campaign he had promised to withdraw U.S. troops
from Iraq, the administration of George W. Bush had declared a date
when the soldiers would leave.

In Afghanistan, allied war planners preparing the 2002 invasion
had expected a more irregular resistance. The Taliban who ran the
country were more militia than a conventionally organized army,
more AK-47 than Main Battle Tank (though they did have a few
tanks, at least before the allied airstrikes began). Their tactics had been
honed in decades of fighting against other Afghan militias and conventional military forces during the Soviet occupation in the 1980s.

Adept at ambush and hit-and-run attacks, the Taliban fighters
were extremely hardy and able to endure long periods without logis-
tical support. After trekking over Afghanistan's harsh terrain, they
would launch an attack with RPGs and machine guns, and occasionally a heavier weapon like a mortar or small artillery piece, then melt
away into the unforgiving countryside. The Taliban were not known,

however, to use suicide attacks. During the Soviet occupation of Afghanistan, there were no known instances of such tactics, except very occasionally by foreign mujahideen fighters, some of whom later became infamous as Al Qaeda.

When I was posted to Afghanistan as a diplomat shortly after the allied invasion, the defenses of our embassy reflected this assessment of the Taliban's military capabilities. The embassy was located in a compound surrounded by high, thick walls. Atop the walls was another high fence of sturdy netting, designed to prevent the flight of RPGs into the compound.

In the early days, during and after the allied invasion, this military assessment proved correct. But after a while, as in Iraq, things began to change. The harbinger had taken place on September 9, 2001, an event overshadowed by the attacks shortly afterward in Washington and New York. Suicide bombers posing as a television film crew assassinated the anti-Taliban mujahideen leader, Ahmed Shah Massoud. Setting up the camera to film him, the "cameraman" blew himself up, and fatally wounded Massoud, who died a few hours later. Indicative of the changing and multinational nature of that conflict, the bombers were Tunisian; the camera had been stolen in Grenoble, France.

There were other antecedents. The Tamil Tigers used suicide attacks extensively against the Sri Lankan army (and, sometimes, civilians) in their fight for a separate Tamil homeland in northern Sri Lanka. Hezbollah cadres used bomb-laden cars and explosive-bearing individuals to attack Israeli army patrols and convoys during Israel's occupation of southern Lebanon. To those watching elsewhere, the technique appeared crucial in dislodging an enemy which otherwise enjoyed a massive military advantage: Israel's conventional strength in tanks and aircraft was far superior to Hezbollah's. Israel withdrew from Lebanon in 2000, demoralized by the suicide attacks it could not effectively prevent.

But it was the suicide attacks in Iraq that seemed to have the most influence. As such attacks mounted in Iraq and increased the discomfort of the allies, suicide attacks became more frequent in Afghanistan, where before they had barely featured. Allied troops, and even trucks carrying humanitarian supplies, were forced to form convoys, protected by tanks and armored vehicles. Not a single major road was safe to travel.

In both Iraq and Afghanistan, the use of suicide bombings produced its own consequences. American and allied forces were forced to adopt aggressive defensive tactics to prevent attacks, including challenging, shooting and destroying people or vehicles that approached allied patrols too closely and ignored (or failed to hear or understand) the warnings given them.

The consequences of these tactics can be imagined and were realized in civilian deaths and growing antipathy to "the occupiers." Eleven members of the same Iraqi family were shot dead in their car approaching coalition troops, just days after the first suicide attack in March 2003.[3] The effects on the troops obliged to adopt these tactics can also be imagined. As in Iraq, debates grew about the wisdom of a long-term allied military presence in Afghanistan. One reason for the spread of the technique of suicide attacks was all too clear: It worked.

This was a new phenomenon. Normally, the deployment of particular military techniques—aerial bombing, mass armored assault—was a function of hardware: the availability of tanks or aircraft, and carefully constructed strategy. These factors themselves are functions of others: economic development and the degree of organization within both the military and society as a whole. The spread of suicide bombings was different. They were spreading like a virus. If their appearance was correlated with anything, it was the degree not of economic development or military organization, but of their opposites.

Some analysts suggest that common to suicide attackers is their strategic objective to remove occupiers from desired territory;[4] some that religious ideology, and in particular Salafi jihadism, is the driving force.[5] Whatever the debate about motives, there is agreement that the incidence of suicide attacks has dramatically increased everywhere over the last two decades, and particularly the last few years. Suicide attacks were not confined to religiously motivated terrorist groups like Hezbollah, the Taliban or Al Qaeda; in Turkey's Kurdish regions and Sri Lanka, the technique was used by groups driven primarily by secular, and indeed nationalist, ideology.[6] Whatever the motivation, the empirical results—of casualties caused, and political effects in consequence—were demonstrable.

This recent trend had earlier precedents. Japan employed kamikaze attacks only during the last stages of the Pacific war, when all chance of strategic victory had evaporated. The Japanese leadership did, however, encourage the attacks, after initial experiment, for the very same reason: They worked. During battles such as that in Leyte Gulf, the U.S. Navy lost scores of vessels to kamikaze attacks. A later survey showed that kamikaze missions were four to five times more likely than conventional missions to damage or sink their targets.[7]

Just as today's suicide attackers are often characterized as fanatical and therefore irrational, the kamikazes have been similarly dismissed as the product of death-loving samurai cultlike thinking that gripped the Japanese military elites. But for them, too, there was a logic: The higher the price exacted upon U.S. forces approaching the Japanese homeland, the more, they hoped, America would hesitate to attack the home islands, and would instead sue for a peace more favorable to Japan. Just as in Iraq, Lebanon and now Afghanistan, suicide attacks were permitted by a culture that celebrated death in combat, but also, and above all, because they had a palpable and successful political effect.

By 2005, the use of suicide bombings had spread to Bali and Britain, which suffered major suicide attacks on the London Underground and buses that year. The U.S. of course had already seen such attacks on September 11, 2001. In Mumbai in 2009, suicide attackers killed nearly two hundred people and wounded more than three hundred in a three-day rampage of shooting and murder. Suicide attacks are now commonplace across North Africa and the Middle East, Pakistan and the Horn of Africa, and have spread elsewhere, including sub-Saharan Africa, Turkey, the Caucasus, Indonesia and the Indian subcontinent and even Iran, where in 2010 suicide bombers killed thirty-nine people.

DESPICABLE AS SOME may find it, suicide bombing has been perhaps the most influential political-military technique of the late twentieth and early twenty-first centuries: In conflicts that are about different ideologies, territories and religions, fighters have adopted the technique without prejudice. In its horror, suicide bombing offers up an insight into something important, something about how change happens, and how we as people work, and thus how things might be changed for the better—but without killing people. Curiously, that lesson is apparent too in sports stadiums.

At many a baseball game, it takes only one or a small group to stand and raise their arms in an attempt to start a wave (they may whoop or cheer at that point). Sometimes the attempt is ignored, but at other times it might initiate a coordinated yet spontaneous motion of tens of thousands of people around the stadium. It's frivolous, fun, but also oddly moving: "We're in this together."

In his book *Herd*, marketing guru Mark Earls explains why people buy what they do, or rather, how they are influenced by the person sitting—or whooping—next to them. Earls cites the sales phenomenon of the Apple iPod. He describes how the color of the headphone cable was a crucial factor in the device's dramatic sales success. The unusual white color of the cords attracted people's attention—and enabled them for once to see the brand choices of their peers even though the product itself remained hidden: The cables made the otherwise private choice visible. The innovative features of the product were of course a vital factor in the ultimate decision to buy the iPod, but it was the white cords that triggered the chain of events that led to the purchase.

Earls suggests that most of our lives are quotations from the lives of others, as Oscar Wilde put it, a phenomenon evident in the spread of agricultural mechanization across America's Midwest in the late nineteenth and early twentieth centuries, when farmers bought tractors when they saw their neighbors had them; or in the names we give our children and the music we listen to. All of these trends, Earls asserts, are shaped by social influence first and foremost, and not by our own independent decisions or the inherent appeal of the thing being chosen.

Hitherto, economic theory has suggested that rational choice—a weighing up of the costs and benefits—is the primary basis for decision making, and particularly purchase decisions. But it turns out that nothing more complicated than mimicry may be a better explanation of why people buy what they do. As one correspondent to the *New Scientist* put it, man should not be named *Homo sapiens*, "wise man," but *Homo mimicus*, "copying man."

? but what about the first + more importantly the second.

Conventional economic theory claims that humans calculate by numbers, assessing rationally the profit and loss of any transaction. But it appears that even in deciding our finances, like taking on or abandoning a mortgage, the behavior of others is influential. The herdlike popularity of subprime mortgages is already well documented. More recently, the practice of abandoning properties whose mortgages cost more than the value of the house has spread "like a contagion," according to a recent study, as both its economic rationale and, crucially, its social acceptability have grown: "It's okay to walk away."[8] Researchers found that borrowers were 23 percent more likely to default on their mortgage once their neighbors had done the same.

This mechanism is evident elsewhere. The British government commissioned research to find out how to persuade people to adopt more pro-environment behavior, for example to limit their carbon emissions. The research found that government was itself an ineffective device to encourage behavioral change: People did not trust government and believed it was using climate arguments as an excuse simply to raise taxes.[9] (Indeed, this distrust is one reason why government may be ineffective in promoting the change necessary to protect the environment.) Instead, the research found, the government would need to recruit more influential agents to persuade people to act. These were not scientists, officials or experts, all of whom were nevertheless more trusted than government. Those with the most potential to influence others' behavior were, the researchers concluded, our next-door neighbors. Indeed, it appears from another study that people take more notice of each other's actions than they do of formal rules.

Researchers at the University of Groningen in the Netherlands tried to see whether the well-known "broken-windows theory" of policing actually worked: the concept that if police aggressively target minor crime, such as littering and vandalism, they will reduce overall lawlessness, including major crime, like assault and mugging.[10] The researchers ran various experiments to find out how context—the environment people encounter—affects behavior, including law-breaking. The researchers were trying to understand how disorderly behavior spreads.

In one experiment, they tested whether people took more notice of a clear legal prohibition—a police sign telling people not to lock their bicycles at a particular spot—or of whether other people were violating the rule by locking their own bicycles there. To test this, they ran scenarios with and without the sign, and the presence or absence of other rule-violators: people illegally locking their bikes.

The study's results were clear. People were more inclined to violate the rule and lock their bicycles illegally if they saw others doing the same thing, regardless of what the police sign said. The study's authors suggest that their evidence therefore confirms the broken-windows theory. As such, the study could be taken as affirmation of an assertive policing model where police act quickly and robustly to deal with minor violations, and thus deter more serious crime. But the study also implies a more subversive message. The Groningen experiments show that norms are more important than rules: It is the *actions* of other people that have the most influence on what we do.

Earls offers the wave as a metaphor for this model of change—it is also in its way an example. It takes no instruction or authority to initiate the rolling wave of spectators standing up and lifting their arms at a sports stadium. One or two people might try to start a wave. If others around them follow, the wave can quickly ripple around the stadium, involving tens of thousands of people in an utterly spontaneous yet coordinated act. The point is a clear one: The

THE LEADERLESS REVOLUTION

person most important in influencing change may be the person standing right next to you.

Suicide bombing and the wave thus offer strikingly similar lessons in how to affect others. Intriguingly, both suggest that it is action in the microcosmos, our own little universe, that matters most: what we *do*. This is not the only parallel.

First, neither suicide bomber nor waver looks to anyone else, let alone their government, to produce the desired effect. Simply, if you want to start a wave, you do not wait for someone else to stand up. More starkly, the suicide bomber is prepared to sacrifice his own body and existence to attack his enemy. Horrible though it may be, it is truly a politics of personal and direct action.

Second, the action is directly linked to the desired effect—in fact, the action *is* that effect. Standing up in your stadium seat, though a small action in a crowd of thousands, constitutes the start of a wave. In contrast, voting for a wave to be started most emphatically does *not* constitute the start of a wave. Detonating a bomb that kills your opponents, as well as yourself as the necessary adjunct, may be viewed by many of us as unconscionable, but it does constitute resistance in a very material and—often—effective manner. Action and consequence are connected without intermediation.

Third, both suicide bombing and waves can plausibly be replicated by others; indeed, in the case of the wave, that is the very point. One reason why suicide bombing has proven so effective is that it requires very little training to undertake and is relatively cheap compared to other military tactics: Others can easily imitate the tactic. An uneducated peasant can suicide-bomb as effectively as an experienced infantryman. Indeed, it would be a waste of a trained soldier to expend him so.

Fourth, the action offers the possibility of real and immediate

To start a
Wave, does take
"Guts"
Most people don't
want to stand
out in a crowd.

change. The wave, if initiated at all, is initiated *immediately*. This must be very satisfying to the person who stands up to start it (I have never done this). Suicide bombers, if successful, will destroy the enemy vehicle or the people being targeted. Though suicide bombers will die in the process, the effect they seek is as immediately forthcoming as their own death.

And in one crucial respect, of course, suicide bombers and wavers are very different. Unless coerced, which they sometimes are, suicide bombers are motivated by a belief (some would call it fanaticism) so great that they are willing to sacrifice their lives. This too helps explain the uniquely persuasive power of suicide bombing. Along with the bomb belts portending the deaths of themselves and their victims, suicide bombers carry something else, undeniably: conviction.

And here is where we must abandon the example of the wave as too superficial, for however fun, few would be much impressed by the conviction of those participating in a wave. And it is conviction that convinces.

Suicide bombers illustrate this truth with horrific violence, but others—Gandhi, American civil rights protesters—have shown the uniquely persuasive force of nonviolence. In either case, it was conviction that propelled the action; it was the action that recruited others to the cause. Thus, an essential first step to produce any lasting influence and change is the discovery of conviction.

This discovery is sometimes a personal realization; sometimes it is conducted with others. For Gandhi, it began in South Africa when as a "colored" he was thrown off a whites-only train. In Alabama in 1955, fifteen-year-old Claudette Colvin was riding the bus home from school when the driver demanded that she give up her seat for a middle-aged white woman, even though three other seats in the row were empty. Claudette Colvin refused to budge. As she put it,

"If she sat down in the same row as me, it meant I was as good as her."[11]

Colvin was arrested. Two police officers, one of them kicking her, dragged her off the bus and handcuffed her. On the way to the police station, they took turns trying to guess her bra size. Colvin's action took place six months before the same was done by Rosa Parks, whose refusal and arrest are the more celebrated, but together their actions triggered a bus boycott. The court case that was occasioned by the boycott, at which Claudette Colvin testified, effectively ended bus segregation. As David Garrow, a biographer of Martin Luther King, Jr., commented, "It's an important reminder that crucial change is often ignited by very plain, unremarkable people who then disappear."[12] *True but there are lots of acts that result in negative outcomes for people.*

Interestingly, network researchers have found similar effects. Contrary to some recent popular books, such as *The Tipping Point*, it is not necessarily a few key influencers who create viral trends; it can be anyone.* In fact, Duncan Watts has found that predicting who is influential in starting or shaping any particular trend is more or less impossible. This may be bad news for advertisers trying to save money by targeting their campaigns to a few key influencers, but in terms of political change, it is very exciting. Anyone can initiate a profound social change. *Yes, but money will try before it succeeds.*

Whatever the insights of network theory or marketing gurus, political change is rather different from buying iPods or downloading the latest Lady Gaga single. Our beliefs about right and wrong are powerfully held; to shift the convictions of others requires profound

---

*In this book, itself influential, Malcolm Gladwell suggests that a few highly connected people influence the choices of everyone else, by what he calls the "Law of the Few." Another book—*The Influentials*—similarly claims that "one American in 10 tells the other 9 how to vote, where to eat, and what to buy."

experience or equal if not more powerful conviction, something rather more substantial than clicking "like" on a Facebook page. In a word, *action*.

These forces are rather harder to measure, though somehow we can tell when such experience strikes or when we are moved by the actions of others: You know it when you see it. Conviction can be found in myriad different ways, but it can rarely be told: As in all good theater, it is better *shown*.

To find true political conviction, beliefs that move us and others must be tested, lived, embodied, just as suicide bombers, horribly, embody theirs. And for this to happen, it's necessary first to confront a painful reality.

It is comforting to believe that governments can provide for us and protect us. Governments want us to believe it, and we want to believe them. Unfortunately, it is ever more evident that this comfortable pact between us rests upon weak foundations indeed.

2

THE PACT

When a child is born in Britain, as in most other developed countries, the parents must register the birth. It is not made clear why this is necessary, but it is legally obligatory. At the local council website, it is politely explained that a new parent is required to register a birth; it is not stated—anywhere—*why*. You are, however, told that you will receive—free of charge!—a short birth certificate. Failure to register a birth is a criminal offense, and can incur a hefty penalty.

It is an ornate and archaic ritual. The harried parent must put aside diapers and bottles in order to attend the local register office, which can be many miles distant. When the appointment takes place, the registrar will enter parents' and child's details into a thick ledger, a book weighty with portentousness. In my case, the registrar had a bulbous fountain pen with which to inscribe the birth date, location and other minutiae. She took an evident pleasure in wielding this instrument, carefully unscrewing the cap and lovingly poising the pen above the thick vellum page for a second, the better for her, and me, to contemplate the gravity of the registration moment.

In Britain, government first instructed its subject populace to register births, deaths and marriages in 1538. The purpose then, of course, was to monitor the population in order to maximize the collection of tax. Today, if it is stated at all, the implied rationale for such registration is the protection of the citizen.

The presence of government at these cardinal moments of life— its beginning, its end, the entwining of one's life with another in marriage—is rarely questioned, but assumed. In this way, government inserts itself into the very foundation and fabric of our lives. With self-assessed taxes, the individual is required to declare to government almost every significant event of their lives.

Reading the registration form for my children (they are twins), I noticed an odd question: Was the child, at birth, alive or dead? I questioned the registrar. She confirmed that, indeed, parents of stillborn children are required to register their births. The deadline—six weeks—is the same as for the births of living children. If the parents of a dead child do not meet that deadline, they too must pay a fine.

"WE ARE THE ONES we've been waiting for" was a compelling slogan from the presidential election campaign of Barack Obama. It captured something about his promise of change, but also, more subtly, spoke to our deeper anxieties about the troubled state of democracy today. It yoked these two ideas together to evoke, in eight words, the suggestion that collective mass action by us could alter things at last. The problem, however, is that the slogan contains a profound but unaddressed contradiction: Even led by a man as enlightened and sophisticated as Barack Obama, government is *not* about mass collective action; only getting someone elected is.

During the campaign, Barack Obama gave a speech in a sports stadium in Denver. Invesco Field, named after its corporate sponsor, had been chosen over other smaller venues in anticipation of the enormous demand to hear him. Only John F. Kennedy had managed to fill a stadium at such a moment. This time, over eighty thousand people filled Invesco Field, while thousands of others watched on huge video screens outside the stadium and millions watched the event on television around the world.

The New York Times published an extraordinary panoramic picture of the stadium crowd, composed of several shots taken over a short period.[1] The picture deserves iconic status: It has an almost religious quality, like a fresco on a cathedral ceiling. The photograph shows a vast and diverse crowd, young and old, black and white: an astonishingly vivid snapshot of Americans animated as never before in this generation by the election of one man, the first African-American with a chance at the presidency, the first Democrat after eight years of George Bush's Republicanism. The picture is moving and awe-inspiring, a visual testament to the political energy and enthusiasm Obama's candidacy unleashed.

During Obama's campaign, reportedly over a million people volunteered to work for his election. This was a larger number than recorded for any previous campaign. Obama raised $650 million for his campaign, the largest amount ever raised; and also, significantly, from the greatest number of donors. However, only a small proportion of Obama's funding came from small individual donors. The vast bulk of the largest donations, as usual with contemporary politics, came from the rich and corporate donors, including banks and corporations like Goldman Sachs, Microsoft, Citigroup and Google.[2]

After his election, the Obama administration, following traditional Washington form, appointed more than two dozen of the largest donors to the Democratic presidential campaign to choice overseas ambassadorships.

The Denver crowd and the extraordinary mass effort mobilized by Obama's campaign spoke of a hunger for change and a willingness to contribute to it without precedent. The enthusiasm did not end with his election: An astonishing ninety thousand people applied for the three thousand or so political appointments in his administration.

Epitomized in the slogan "Yes, we can," Obama's campaign played upon people's desire for change as well as, crucially, for *involvement* in politics. Both during the campaign and since, Obama urged people to become involved in their communities, to volunteer and themselves help fulfill the political promise of his election. But in this message there was unadmitted contradiction. For what Obama was asking for, first and foremost, was not for volunteers to improve their communities, but for volunteers to campaign for his election. As if to highlight this awkward fusion of objectives, one group—Obama Works—was set up for people to volunteer for local activities in the name of Obama's campaign. Obama's campaign call to local action was a secondary if necessary moral buttress to his primary appeal for voters' support. The political end of his campaign was not change itself, but for him to be *elected* to deliver change—a subtle but crucial distinction, and the disjunction at the heart of representative democracy.

The night of Obama's election, a great roar could be heard across Lower Manhattan when his victory became apparent. But the party atmosphere soon dissipated. After Obama's election and the excitement of his inauguration, you could almost sense the air going out of the balloon.

With the government's encouragement, volunteering fairs were held across the country. And while attendance was high, it was noted that this enthusiasm was less a function of a new surge of political activism, but more one of the rampant unemployment of the post-election months. In Brooklyn, a few hundred turned up to a volunteering fair, where thousands had been hoped for—in a borough numbering millions. Tellingly, the fair was described as seeking to exploit energy "left over" from the campaign.[3] Obama Works went into "hibernation." Since then, there has been no revolution in volunteering and community organizing. The conventional model of politics has remained largely unchanged. As usual, attention focuses on the intentions and utterances of a very small group of people in the White House and a slightly larger group in Congress, where the betrayals, ethos and peccadilloes of a small number of representatives and senators determine the nature of legislation imposed on a country of three hundred million people. Everyone else is left to rant about their doings on websites or, more commonly, simply get on with their lives with a shrug of the shoulders. It seems like the ones we've been waiting for wasn't us after all.

Some attribute this passivity to the inherently idle and feckless nature of ordinary people: Some politicians I know are inclined to this supposition. But in truth, the reason is that conventional representative democracy, where the many elect the few, rests on a pact between voters and government: We vote, they act; we get on with our lives, they protect. This is the pact in which the parent must enroll their baby after birth. It endures until death. This pact is rarely examined, and nowhere is it clearly or fully stated; it is rarely admitted to, though its effects are profound.

The pact has several layers. At the most fundamental, the pact implies that government will protect its citizens; it will provide for their security and safety. In return, citizens agree to limit some of their freedom: They accept the rule of law, and with it, various restrictions on their behavior. To government is reserved certain extreme powers and rights, which are denied the rest of us. These include the power to deny freedom to others, to imprison and to punish. In some countries, like the U.S., this includes the power to kill in the name of justice. All 192 member states of the United Nations have agreed to a code to govern this right to wage war, the UN Charter. But the charter is a voluntary document and infringing it does not invoke automatic punishment, especially if the infringer is a powerful state.

Domestically, the government's commitment to provide security means that government takes responsibility to preserve peace, prevent crime and disorder, and to save the populace in times of grave peril, say, after military attack or natural disaster. So far, the pact is familiar, and echoes the theories of political philosophers down the ages, from Locke and Hobbes, and earlier still, Plato.

Less familiar is the second layer of the pact, one that is less often mentioned than the first, but one with more insidious effect. In addition to protecting the population, government makes a further commitment—to take care of society's problems, including education, in some states health care services, care for the elderly and disabled, protection of the natural environment, including now the globe's atmosphere, and above all, providing for growth and employment—to take care of the economy. This commitment—and its consequence—are almost never explicitly stated: Government will take care of these problems, so we don't have to.

Instead of admitting this pact, politicians declare policies and promises to manage these problems, much as Barack Obama did at Invesco Field. But by declaring government's intention to address such problems, a politician is sending a powerful if concealed message: If government is willing and able to sort out these problems, we the populace do not need to worry. In Barack Obama's case, the message was carried a step further: I the politician need your active involvement—to campaign, raise money, etc.—in order to get elected, then I will be able to address these problems.

Indeed, Obama raised the stakes a notch further: The mass involvement he was able to activate through his candidacy exploited the massive political energy and frustration of the progressive elector ate: the millions who volunteered for his campaign. His implicit message was "Mobilize to elect me and I will deliver."

But the effects of the pact can be witnessed in what followed the election. The mass of volunteers who mobilized to campaign for Obama by and large threw away their badges and stayed at home, their job done. There was no dramatic upswing in volunteering for social causes. Even in electoral politics, hard-core party activists found that the "Obama effect" had little long-term benefit in recruiting volunteers to fight elections at the more local level. The long-run trend in volunteering for social causes remains, as Robert Putnam and others have attested, resolutely downward.[4] In general, we are doing less and less. And here is one message that issued unintended but with subtle and powerful force from the millions watching that one charismatic man at Invesco Field. That vast crowd is *watching*, not acting. For most of us, politics is a spectator sport—we observe, they do.

The trouble with the pact is that it is breaking down. National governments are less and less able to tackle the transnational and global causes of the various problems that confront us. At the most basic level of the pact, government is unable to guarantee protection against terrorist attack; it is unable to provide an effective response to prevent climate change; it is unable to manage the global causes—

and effects—of economic volatility. In society, government is unable to slow the seemingly inexorable rise in "antisocial" behavior, a trend evidenced, for example, in mounting attacks on bus drivers, and apparent in other, innumerable ways, including the subtle yet palpable tension in our public spaces. CCTV cameras on every corner do little to curb this discomforting trend, though they provide ample proof of our absence of trust in one another.

As a result, trust in politicians, never high, is declining. In Britain, a well-known television presenter called the prime minister "a cunt" in front of a studio audience. Such disrespect is now commonplace in many established democracies. In America and virtually every democratic country, there is widespread disillusionment if not disgust with the political classes, and with politics itself. In Germany, polling before recent Bundestag (parliament) elections indicated that 18 percent of voters would vote not for regular politicians but for a comedian playing a politician.[5] The election campaign was dominated not by discussion of education or economic policy, but by a scandal over a politician who had used her government car to be driven on holiday to Spain. Commenting on elections widely seen as "boring," one voter said, "There's just no belief that anything is going to change."[6] In Iceland, widespread disillusionment after the catastrophic impact of the financial crisis saw a professional comic elected mayor of Reykjavík. In the U.S., antipathy toward politicians manifests itself mostly, as in most issues in America, in partisan terms: The other side's politicians are venal, corrupt and self-serving; the manifest failings of ours are overlooked.

The disintegration of the pact is exacerbated by a further damaging phenomenon: the deepening chasm between voters and their representatives. The evolution of democracy has been, in general, from direct to representative, from people's collectively deciding their affairs to their electing others to decide on their behalf. But as representative democracy has evolved, so too has the distance grown between voters and the decisions affecting them.

In every national democratic system, individual participation has been reduced to mere occasional voting to choose legislators or the executive (in the British system, these are one and the same election; in the U.S. and other systems, they are separated). Today, the executive, in cahoots with the legislature, manages society and the economy and the country's international affairs. These highly complex decisions are taken not by the population collectively, but by a small executive often comprising only a few hundred people. This pyramidal, top-down structure produces several inherent and thus inescapable features.

The competition to become one of the elite is intense and antagonistic, and sometimes violent. It costs an estimated $1.5 million to win a seat in the U.S. House of Representatives; in the Senate, $9 million.[7] Once in power, legislators join lobbyists in ferocious competition to gain the executive's attention and influence their decisions. The evidence for this is clear in the growing professionalization of this process, both of politicians and the industry established to influence them. In Britain, many politicians have spent their whole professional lives practicing nothing but politics, starting as researchers to Members of Parliament, then graduating as MPs and sometimes government ministers. David Cameron, elected Britain's prime minister in 2010, has never had any job outside of politics, unless one counts a brief stint working in public relations. The leader of the opposition, Ed Miliband, likewise. In Washington, every politician claims to be an "outsider" as they try to ride the antipolitics wave, but in reality very few are.

The contest to secure political influence has become increasingly professionalized and has assumed the characteristics of an industry, with professional associations and its own group interests: There are now lobbyists representing the interests of lobbyists. In Washington, the number of registered lobbyists has more than doubled since 2000, to nearly thirty-five thousand in 2005.[8] While the recession may have thinned their ranks, the ratio of lobbyists to legislators remains, incredibly, hundreds of lobbyists to every member of Congress.

At the European Union in Brussels, an increasingly dominant source of legislation affecting economic interests worldwide, no one seems able to give precise numbers of professional lobbyists; most estimates, though, place the number at about fifteen thousand. A former commissioner for the EU's most expensive and wasteful policy, agriculture, described Brussels as a "paradise" for lobbyists.

One reason for the proliferation of business lobbyists is all too clear: It pays to invest in influence. BP helped Liberal Democrat European Parliament member Chris Davies draft climate change legislation that secured a €9 billion subsidy from European taxpayers, covering the entire cost of new technology to convert from "dirty" coal-fired power stations, saving energy firms from having to pay for it themselves. The industry later gave Davies an award. Davies was at least open about the process he conducted to prepare the new European laws, justifying his actions by using a famous quotation often misattributed to Otto von Bismarck: "The public should never be allowed to see two things: how sausages are made and how laws are made."[9]

If this is the reality of the supposedly democratic legislative process, it is unsurprising that popular enthusiasm for conventional politics is waning. Membership of political parties, one measure of popular participation in conventional politics, is in steep decline in all major Western societies.[10] Global surveys confirm that while people in general prefer democracy, they are less and less happy with the practice of democratic government.[11] Voter turnout has been in long-term decline in almost all democratic systems. In the last parliamentary elections in France, for instance, turnout was the lowest ever recorded. The European Parliament elections of 2009 suffered the same ignominious outcome—fewer voters turned out for them than in any election since the parliament's inception. In the United States, 25 percent fewer people vote in elections than they did in 1960, when John F. Kennedy was elected.

Despite the promises of politicians to limit the lobbying industry and its influence, it has continued to grow. Its pernicious power—an inherent function of the reductive pyramid from voters to deciders—seems greater than them. One of President Obama's first acts in government was to appoint as deputy defense secretary a longtime lobbyist for Raytheon, a top weapons contractor, despite Obama's campaign commitment to prohibit any such appointments. In New York state, the successful Democratic candidate for governor in 2010 proclaimed his forthright opposition to special interests and lobbyists throughout his campaign, yet the bulk of his campaign funding came from organized labor, real estate firms and related industries like construction, the health care sector and lobbying firms.[12]

In 2010, the Supreme Court, in its misleadingly named "Citizens United" ruling, decided to allow commercial companies to pay directly for political advertising, absurdly defining companies as having the same rights as individuals, and overruling the existing feeble limits to curb their influence. The ruling permitted corporations and other types of organizations to raise large amounts and run political campaign ads without revealing the source of funding. Sure enough, the 2010 congressional elections saw large influxes of money from these unaccountable bodies, tilting the races for many seats. Professor

Lawrence Lessig has argued that the mutual dependency of lobbyists and legislators is now so profound, and corrupt, that legislation is enacted with the sole purpose of extracting rents from corporate interests. Former senators have admitted the same thing: that all legislation is made on "K Street," the infamous Washington address where lobbyists have their offices.[13] One observer estimates that the lobbying industry spent $3.3 billion in just one year (2008).[14] Private companies that run prisons now employ lobbyists to press for legislation requiring judges to impose longer sentences.[15]

In Britain, the corrosive influence of lobbyists is better concealed and less acknowledged. In a system where vast power is concentrated in the prime minister's office, many of Tony Blair's advisers left office for highly paid executive positions in companies that had substantial political interests in their earlier incarnation. One senior adviser joined Morgan Stanley's investment banking division as a full-time senior managing director. Another left her job in Blair's inner team to work for the oil giant BP.

Several of Blair's press advisers formed a PR group on Blair's departure from office that now enjoys lucrative contracts with businesses, many of which had clear interests in legislation delivered by the Blair administration. After leaving office, Blair himself was awarded a position as "senior adviser" to investment bank JPMorgan for a salary of half a million pounds a year, a role to which he gave rather less publicity than to his position as a peace envoy in the Middle East for the so-called Quartet group of countries.

WITHIN THE POLITICAL CLASS in Britain, there appears to be a tacit understanding not to criticize such obvious conflicts of interest, perhaps because some members of that class wish to leave themselves that opportunity in future. The self-serving excuse, which can often be heard sotto voce in Westminster, is that such rewards are a just payoff for the supposedly poor pay and hard labor of a career in politics.

A similar unspoken understanding is clearly at work in Washington too, where politicians "retire" from their legislative duties as elected officials to sell their contacts and networking expertise as lobbyists. When former Democratic majority leader Senator Tom Daschle was scrutinized by Congress to lead President Obama's health care effort, it was revealed that he had earned over $5 million as a lobbying adviser to various industries. Notably, it was not this blatant influence-peddling that provoked the criticism that met his nomination, and ultimately forced him to withdraw, but his failure accurately to declare for taxes the gratis use of a limousine—one client's form of payment for his services.

Meanwhile, former American ambassadors, after their years of public service, sometimes return to Washington to act as paid lobbyists for the very countries to which they used to represent U.S. interests, a naked breach of ethics, not to speak of the risk to national security.[16] Two senior officials from the Clinton administration, including the former president's legal counsel, later ended up as paid lobbyists for Laurent Gbagbo, the former president of Côte d'Ivoire, whose refusal to relinquish power after losing elections in 2011 led to widespread violence costing hundreds of lives. These well-connected American officials lobbied the State Department and White House on behalf of the worst of tin-pot dictators.[17]

GIVEN THE PERNICIOUS FORCES at work in the current political system, it is unsurprising that the decisions produced are often grossly divorced from the needs of electors, or even of the state itself. In the United States, where the lobbying industry is most developed and where politicians are highly dependent on campaign contributions, these effects are most noticeable. For instance, members of Congress in 2009 demanded that the government purchase seven extra F-22 fighter aircraft, at nearly a quarter of a billion dollars each, which the Department of Defense itself had not requested. At this point, the U.S. was at war in two countries—Iraq and Afghanistan. Although by that time already in USAF service, the F-22 had not been used in either conflict. In the UK, the government has been convinced by the defense industry to purchase two enormous aircraft carriers to "maintain Britain's ability to project force," even though the carriers offer a far greater capability than Britain has enjoyed for many decades, if not ever.

Trade sanctions are commonly instituted by the U.S. to pressure countries that have committed some grievous breach of international peace and security, or stand accused of "state sponsorship" of terrorism, like Iraq, Libya or Iran. Some American companies, however, have managed to win exemptions to rules preventing trade with these countries. Unsurprisingly, most are large companies with a commensurate lobbying presence in Washington. Kraft Foods, Pepsi and some of the nation's largest banks have secured thousands of exemptions for their products to be sold to countries like Iran, allowing them to do billions of dollars of business despite tough measures to prevent commerce with states that sponsor terrorism. Wrigley's chewing gum was classed as "humanitarian aid" and thus exempted from sanctions, permitting millions of dollars of sales to Iran and other sanctioned countries. One official later admitted that while the government debated whether chewing gum counted as food, and thus would be exempt, lobbyists too had played their part: "We were probably rolled on that issue by outside forces."[18]

On another patch of the carpet, the oil giant BP revealed that it had "expressed concern" to the British government about slow progress in diplomatic negotiations between Libya and Britain on the transfer of prisoners, on the grounds that it might negatively affect BP's oil exploration contracts with the Libyan government. These contracts were worth $900 million. The company claimed that such an expression, and indeed its concern, had nothing to do with the incarceration of the Lockerbie bomber Abdelbaset al-Megrahi, whom Libya was campaigning to have transferred to Libya from his Scottish prison, where he had been sentenced to life imprisonment for the 1988 bombing, which killed two hundred seventy people.

BP admitted its intervention on the prisoner exchange issue only after al-Megrahi's transfer to Libya and following a public outcry. The delay in the negotiation had been caused by the British government's insistence that the Lockerbie bomber be excluded from the prisoner transfer agreement. It backed down, and no exclusion to the agreement was specified. Al-Megrahi was transferred, much to the outrage of many of the families of those killed.

Thanks to pressure from lobbyists and agricultural special interests, the U.S. Department of Agriculture has spent millions of dollars, under both Republican and Democratic administrations, encouraging the consumption of cheese, including the promotion of extra-cheese Domino's pizzas which contain 40 percent more cheese than "regular" pizzas. Pressing this foodstuff upon consumers is directly contrary to the interests of citizens themselves, whose consumption of cheese, and with it saturated fat, has tripled over the last thirty years. Other parts of the government, including the Agriculture Department's own nutrition committee, meanwhile, are busy telling Americans to reduce their consumption of highly saturated fats.[19] Perversely, the government's promotion of cheese is a direct consequence of consumers' growing preference for low-fat and nonfat milk and dairy products. This has created vast surpluses of whole milk and milk fat, which the dairy industry turned to the government to help offload— as high-fat cheese. Thus, even as consumers exercise their own choice to eat less fat, the government, pressured by cheese lobbyists (hilarious but true), exploits the consequence—unused high-fat milk and cheese—to persuade the consumer to eat more of it.

In a similar case in Britain, the government in 2011 published a list of healthy eating guidelines, including the advice that consumers should eat no more than 2.5 ounces of red and processed meat per day. The Department of Health produced a list helpfully indicating several meaty items alongside their respective weights. Alongside a cooked breakfast and the Sunday roast and other common meals, only two branded products were mentioned by name: Big Mac and Peperami. It just so happened that both items came in under the limit. The previous November the government had set up five "responsibility deal" networks with the food business to come up with health policies. At the time, this was criticized as being akin to letting Big Tobacco draft smoking policy. Two of the companies were McDonald's and Unilever, who happen to be the manufacturers of the Big Mac and Peperami, respectively.[20]

THE POLITICAL SPACE is occupied more and more not by citizens, but by big business and the wealthy. Not content with the purchase of lobbying power in our nations' capitals, oil companies are using the political techniques of environmental activists to promote their own interests, in this case to prevent curbs on carbon emissions. In a memo leaked in 2009, the American Petroleum Institute, which represents the U.S. oil industry, wrote to its member companies asking them to "move aggressively" to stage up to twenty-two "Energy Citizen" gatherings, mostly located, it turned out, in districts of representatives with slim majorities. Without irony, the memo declared that the objective of the demonstrations, which would be organized and funded by API, would be to "put a human face" on the impacts of "unsound" energy policy, i.e., efforts to limit climate change.

Elsewhere, wealthy philanthropists use their foundations, and financial pull, to promote their political preferences. The foundation of Wall Street billionaire and Nixon administration commerce secretary Peter G. Peterson, for instance, is seeking to address the issue of taxes, deficits and fiscal responsibility, using advertising and public appearances by foundation experts to educate the public and increase engagement on the issue of the fiscal deficit. The foundation's website offers sample op-ed articles and letters to public officials and editors, some of which have appeared in newspapers. All members of Congress received a copy of a report by the foundation.[21] This is an interesting twist on the traditional understanding of philanthropy; some foundations now act—with tax-free benefits—as a kind of "force multiplier" for the political preferences of the "philanthropist." These activities may be beneficent, such as Bill Gates's efforts to improve school curriculums, or malignant, but either form of influence shares one common characteristic—it is accountable to no one.

It is not only big business that engages in the lobbying business. To compete in the overcrowded and cacophonous halls of modern "democratic" legislatures, anyone with an axe to grind has to follow the same tactics. At international conferences, invariably there are now "NGO forums" to accommodate the scores and sometimes

hundreds—as at the Copenhagen climate conference—of organizations with views to present. There is no assessment of the democratic
legitimacy of these groups: Some represent many millions of members; others are tiny, and represent nobody apart from themselves.
The more skillful use direct tactics to get their message across to
legislators: The National Rifle Association, one of the most accomplished at this practice, maintains an online roster of the voting
patterns of members of Congress, "scoring" them according to their
support of—or hostility to—pro-gun positions. Such tactics are now
becoming commonplace across the political spectrum.

The number of nonprofits in the U.S. has increased by over
30 percent between 1996 and 2008, to well over 1.5 million.[22] Such
organizations are today more likely to be located in Washington and
have a subscriber base of members who pay dues but do not attend
or participate in local meetings. There have been similar trends in
Britain. Such organizations are in effect turning political activity into
a business, what some have called a "business of protest." The orga-
nizational model for many contemporary political nonprofit organizations now resembles that of a commercial business, which defines
its target audience, purchases relevant mailing lists and advertising
to reach that audience, and asks minimal participation (usually just
membership fees) from them to achieve their lobbying goals.[23]
Whereas active participation in community organizations correlates
with political participation, there are no such "positive externalities"
of paying membership dues to a nonprofit. In essence, we are contracting out politics to be done by others.

Common to these interest groups is that they are in general fo-
cused on single, narrow issues: gun rights, fuel taxes, environmental
protection, abortion rights. Their aggressive tactics and sheer numbers fill the domestic political space and have created a new culture

of politics, where legislators are confronted with a panoply of groups and lobbyists, erecting a kind of wall between them and individual voters.

Such groups also contribute to a growing and unpleasant extremism in political debate. Adept at one-sided presentation of the evidence, these groups advocate black-and-white positions with aggressive vigor and armfuls of one-sided research—often representing those who oppose them as foolish and sometimes evil. The compromises inherently necessary in political decision making thus become harder; deadlock becomes likelier. Facts and reasoned analysis are invariably the victims.

One effect of these trends is the polarizing rise of partisanship. Many have commented on the growing ugliness and vituperation of public debate. For the first time in living memory, a lawmaker shouted, "You lie!" at the U.S. president when he spoke to both houses of Congress. It is a long way from the method of the Indian "talking stick," introduced by the Iroquois to Ben Franklin, and reportedly used by America's Founding Fathers, which requires participants to be able to articulate one another's position before having a chance to speak.

At the conservative *National Review*, which had prided itself on its high-minded and thoughtful debate, the columnist Kathleen Parker received eleven thousand e-mail messages when she argued in an article during the 2008 presidential campaign that Governor Sarah Palin was unfit to be vice president. One message lamented that her mother did not abort her.[24] On the Internet, which some extol for its invigorating heterogeneity and debate, it is clear that the opposite is also true: Online, people tend to choose views that confirm their own.[25] There are even dating sites to accommodate lonely hearts distinguished by their political views.

In Britain, recent elections saw the first-ever accession to a parliamentary seat—in the European Parliament—of a far-right party with the victory of the British National Party. In the U.S., Republicans and Democrats are increasingly choosing to live apart from one another, and locate themselves with others of similar political views.[26] Red and blue are now more starkly drawn than ever.*

The polarization of political views, the intercession of business, lobbyists and interest groups between voters and their representatives, the growing number and power of political actors who are neither politicians nor conventional political parties, nor accountable to anyone but themselves yet nonetheless wield considerable influence—together, these factors suggest a deepening divide between the public and their nominal representatives. They suggest nothing less than a crisis in democracy.

THE PACT BETWEEN CITIZEN and government is never explicit. You can spend an entire life paying taxes, obeying laws, without once being asked whether you wish to contract into or out of it. Government insists upon your registration at birth, and to be notified upon your death. At no point does it seek your consent. You never get the chance to contract into the pact: Your parents are legally obliged to

---

*Though there is not the space here to explore this phenomenon fully, this sorting—or to put it more bluntly, segregation—by political views, which occurs also according to income, religion and race, is a characteristic of complex systems. Economist Thomas Schelling won the Nobel Prize in economics for explaining how the choice made by a few, say, Democrats, to live in a particular location can, over time, transform or "tip" a hitherto mixed neighborhood into one that is uniformly of one political persuasion. Even if individuals are tolerant at the micro level, over time a neighborhood will become segregated—a phenomenon called "micro level tolerance; macro level segregation."

do so on your behalf whether they like it or not. And there is only one way to contract out.

The pact rests on one central pillar (and oddly, it is the same whether a country is democratic or not)—that government more or less represents the collective interests of the populace. The democratic process provides—in theory at least—for continual feedback, as Karl Popper once theorized, from governed to governors, the only way, he believed, to optimize policy so that it reflects the needs and preferences of the people. But if that feedback is interrupted, government policy, at best approximate to the collective wishes of the people, starts to diverge. People and government become estranged. When this happens, the pact breaks down. The evidence is accumulating in the twenty-first century that this is indeed happening.

If government cannot provide for the stability, safety and just arbitration of our common affairs, who can? The answer is both radical and discomforting. For there is only one alternative if government cannot successfully provide: We must do so ourselves. Self-organized government is one term; another, rather more loaded term, is anarchism.

But this is not the anarchism of early-twentieth-century bomb-wielding Russians, or nihilists charging police lines at G8 summits. It is a different vision, of individuals and groups peacefully organizing their affairs, arbitrating necessary business directly with one another, guided by their conviction and direct experience—not by party political dogma. It is more evolution than revolution, for it is dawning on people across the world that in order to fix our problems, there is no one to look to but ourselves. The minimalist act of voting is looking less and less adequate as a solution.

This vision may animate people, but it does not prescribe. Instead, this new way of doing things is just that—a way of doing things, a method, and emphatically not an end in itself, nor a design to be imposed upon others. Only a fool would wish the abrupt or violent overthrow of the current system, for the certain result would be violent chaos—anarchy of the worst kind.

But if it's true that government is less and less able to manage our collective affairs, it seems we have little choice but to take that burden upon our own shoulders. We must learn anew to look to ourselves to produce the effects we desire, to take responsibility for ourselves and for others, and to cooperate and negotiate with each other, instead of leaving that arbitration to an evidently imperfect mechanism. As these habits spread, a new and more durable order may emerge, not—as now—legislated from above but built from the ground up, by people acting upon their beliefs and engaging with each other.

For curiously, it is perpetuation of the existing way of doing things, not anarchism, that may pose the greater risk to our peace and security. It is the alienation of government from people, and us from each other, that more endangers our fragile stability. It is no coincidence that this is the most common criticism of anarchism, that it engenders disorder, that Anarchy = Chaos. Let us examine this most serious objection to this different way of doing things.

3

ANARCHY = CHAOS

W hen the trouble first ignited in March 2004, I was in Geneva, at a conference designed—ironically, it turned out—to promote reconciliation between Kosovo's Albanians and Serbs. An adviser to Kosovo's prime minister, a friend, drew me aside: "Three Albanian children have been killed," she whispered conspiratorially, "by a Serb." With deliberate portentousness, she added, "There will be trouble." Curiously, she seemed excited by the news, as if relieved that, at last, *something* was happening.

Next day, back in Pristina, Kosovo's capital, where I then lived, it was clear that her premonition was correct.[1] Tension was palpable in that city's polluted air, straining people's faces. The rumors were widespread, amplified by irresponsible journalists: A Serb had driven three children to their deaths, the reporters claimed, by drowning.*

---

*The deaths were later found to have been accidental.

Not only that, but they had died that horrible death in the Ibar, the very river dividing Serb and Albanian halves of Mitrovica, Kosovo's most divided city.

That afternoon, at UN headquarters where I worked, we received reports of crowds gathering in towns and villages across the province. Suddenly, the security guards announced over the office loudspeakers that a large group of young men was approaching the headquarters. Soon, their chanting "U-Ç-K! U-Ç-K! U-Ç-K!"—roughly, Ooh-Chay-Kah—reverberated around the building, loud and aggressive. "UÇK" is the abbreviation for the Kosovo Liberation Army, the Kosovo Albanian guerrillas who resisted Slobodan Milošević's repression, including during the 1999 war that led to the withdrawal of Yugoslav forces.

Without warning, the loudspeakers announced that the building was immediately to be evacuated. But there was no information on how the evacuation should proceed or where the UN staff would go. There was a sudden and anxious sense of panic. People began to run up and down corridors. Mobile phones stopped working—it was later discovered that the riots had overloaded the networks, partly because some had used their phones to organize the riots. For some reason, the elevators stopped functioning too. Some began to weep, perhaps with fear.

I was with my wife, who had come to my office for its greater security. My Albanian assistant, Besnik, took charge and ushered us down the fire escape and into a car. We drove out of the compound and back to our house. On the streets, groups of young people were gathering. Many were children. They looked excited and agitated. That night, the groups merged into mobs.

I had agreed that evening to take part in a television discussion with political leaders at the main television station in Pristina. As we set out driving to the studio, a large mass of people blocked the streets near our house. It was dark and I could not tell their number. The mass swelled and shifted; it had a shape and intent beyond its individual components. There was shouting and the bangs of what I thought at the time were firecrackers. I later realized it was gunfire. There were no police in sight.

The television debate was ugly. Along with an American diplomat, I argued that the riots must stop immediately. Parents should tell their children to go home. But the political leaders from Kosovo's Albanian majority did not agree. According to them, the trouble was the UN's fault. In their version, the riots had been triggered by the UN's decision to allow Serb protesters from a village near Pristina to block one of the main roads to the south.

The Kosovo Albanian leaders argued that the anger on the streets was legitimate protest at the many injustices Kosovars had suffered, past and present. From the tenor and aggression of the debate, it was clear that some of the leaders sensed a revolutionary moment where the UN, the de facto power in Kosovo, might be overthrown. They grasped the tail of the tiger. By the end of the program, my back was in painful spasm from the tension gripping me. I returned home through a city smoldering with violence.

Back at home with some Albanian friends, we sat listening to the gunfire and occasional explosions. A red glow appeared at our window. We looked out to see sparks and flames spurting into the air nearby. We realized it was the Serbian church at the top of our street, aflame. There was an awful sound: a bell ringing incessantly.

After a while, when things seemed calmer, my friend Ardi suggested we go out to see what was going on. We walked up our street to the church. It was ablaze like a summer bonfire, its steeple a column of fire. On top, the church bell rang with a desperate rhythm.

The heat was somehow making it ring. Fortunately, there was no one still inside the blazing building. At last the bell stopped. Scores of young men surrounded the church. Their work done, many were sitting, gazing at the fire, smoking and chatting. Someone was selling cigarettes.

We walked away. Ardi, a Kosovo Albanian, would not look at me. He was beside himself with anger and shame. Spent cases of plastic bullets and rifle cartridges crunched under our feet. The UN riot police had confronted the mob here. But they had been overwhelmed and retreated, leaving the church to its fate. All across Kosovo, the forces of law and order—the UN and local police and NATO peacekeepers—had lost control. In one town, a contingent of German soldiers had remained in barracks while a mob of thousands roamed the town for hours, moving from district to district, picking out Serb churches, houses and UN offices, ransacking buildings and putting them to the torch. When we later visited the town, we saw at its center a blackened hillside, studded with the shells of burnt-out houses, as if a forest fire had swept through it.

The next day, the violence continued. There were reports of buses transporting rioters around the province to attack different Serb enclaves. In southern Kosovo, a large mob was prevented from besieging a Serb Orthodox monastery by the intervention of a local Albanian former KLA guerrilla leader (he was later to become Kosovo's prime minister). In the divided town of Mitrovica, where the Albanian children had drowned, NATO troops shot and killed several Albanians trying to cross the river to attack Serbs in the northern part of the city. Riots went on around the country into the night. Every UN office in the territory was attacked, more than 150 UN vehicles were destroyed. At least 550 homes and twenty-seven Orthodox churches and monasteries were burned, and more than four thousand people—mostly Serbs, but also Roma and other minority groups—were driven from their homes.[2]

Eventually, the violence died down. Local political leaders claimed that their calls to end the turmoil had worked, rarely confessing that these entreaties had been made under pressure from international officials. But in truth it appeared more that the chaos and violence had simply petered out. On the streets, the rhythm and the momentum of the violence pulsed through the city. Before the violence erupted, you could feel it build up as an urge needing expression. As the violence played out, that dark energy was ventilated. As it ended, somehow you could tell that the force that had driven the chaos and rage had at last been exhausted.

IT IS COMMONLY HELD that society requires authority in order to enjoy peace and stability. Without such institutions—law, the police, the army—society will collapse into anarchy and disorder; the many will fall victim to the criminal few. In case we need reminding of what this might be like, movies abound with depictions of anarchy, even if often perpetuated by zombie hordes (*28 Days Later*, *I Am Legend*) or provoked by alien invasion (*War of the Worlds*). Either way, the anarchy shown is entertainingly terrifying. It seems there is only a fragile veil dividing us from the jungle. Television offers ceaseless titillating depiction—both real and falsified—of the criminals who lurk to destroy us, but for the thin blue line of law and order that holds them back.

But in these illustrations lies a clue. There is scant entertainment involved in the real and actual horrors of humanity—the Holocaust, the Khmer Rouge's "Year Zero" or the butchery of Charles Manson. If anarchy were so close, and so awful, we wouldn't find its Hollywood depiction entertaining; instead, we would find it horribly frightening, unwatchable.

One criticism of anarchism as a political strategy is so ubiquitous that it merely requires a reshaping of the word: anarchism = anarchy. Without a superstructure of institutions to maintain order, it is claimed, disorder and chaos will surely result—Hobbes's "war of all against all."

This is indeed a frightening prospect that few dare contemplate. When disaster strikes, like an earthquake in Haiti or a hurricane in New Orleans, it is never long before commentators, safe in their television studios, issue dire warning of social disorder and breakdown, as if this is more frightening than the original natural disaster. In post-Katrina New Orleans, reports of carjackings, rapes and murders flooded the news. Thousands of law enforcement agents were deployed from other states as Louisiana's governor warned, "They have M16s and are locked and loaded. These troops know how to shoot and kill and I expect they will." Police in one suburb neighboring the flooded city were so alarmed at the prospect of looters and other malcontents that they blocked the bridge from the city, preventing the hungry and desperate from getting help. Others coldbloodedly shot fleeing refugees.

As the essayist Fareed Zakaria has noted, the federal government's fastest and most efficient response to Hurricane Katrina was the creation of a Kafkaesque, Guantánamo-like prison facility in which twelve hundred American citizens were summarily detained and denied any of their constitutional rights for months.[3] Later accounts, such as Dave Eggers's *Zeitoun*, told stories ignored at the time, like that of Abdulrahman Zeitoun, who after the hurricane paddled around the flooded city in a canoe offering help, ferrying neighbors to higher ground and caring for abandoned pets, only to be arrested by National Guardsmen and held incommunicado for several weeks without charge and without medical attention along with other Arab-American companions.

But as Rebecca Solnit has written, disasters in fact often produce the opposite of disorder in human society: instead of violence and anarchy, community and solidarity.[4]

A RECENT LETTER to the *Financial Times* makes a common claim: that civilization is fundamentally fragile and requires government to protect it. The correspondent cites the example of the arrival of the mutineers from the *Bounty* on the isolated Pacific island of Pitcairn:

> When the nine Bounty mutineers and 17 Tahitian men and women arrived there in 1789 it was as close to the Garden of Eden as anywhere in the real world: generously endowed with water, sunshine and fertile soils, and uninhabited by anyone else. The perfect test of Hobbes versus Rousseau. In the event, Hobbes won. The British sailors fought among themselves and tried to subjugate the Tahitians. The Tahitians resisted and fought among themselves.
>
> By 1800, 11 years later, only one of the mutineers, nine Tahitian women, and many children were left, most of the others having died unnatural deaths. The surviving mutineer created political order by establishing not just an autocracy but a theocracy, with himself as the link between God and man.[5]

The writer concludes—quite reasonably, given the episode he offers as an example—by emphasizing "the importance of continued efforts to sustain governance organizations that bring together the specific interests that count most in the definition of a common (national, regional, global) interest, in order that, through repeated interaction, convergent interests will prevail over divergent ones."

The writer's conclusion is entirely correct. Unfortunately, however, it is not clear that contemporary political institutions, whether national or international, do in fact successfully give sufficient attention to the common interests of humanity. Instead, it's increasingly evident that these institutions instead elevate the interests of the most powerful interest groups over collective interests, and neglect long-term primary needs, including the environment.

One can also argue that the worst outrages in human history occurred not in the absence of authority and government, but were instead perpetrated by governments claiming to act in the common interest: Nazi Germany, Stalinist Soviet Union, Khmer Rouge Cambodia—the list is a very long one. The criminal acts undertaken by these governments were permitted and in fact ordered in the name of the collective interest; the individual perpetrators were thus rendered immune. Democratic governments are also fully capable of terrible crimes, legitimized by government's ultimate moral immunity of *droit d'état*, or "state interest" (on this, more later). But in any case, the correspondent's argument is widely shared: Institutions protect us against ourselves, above all against what would otherwise prevail—chaos and disorder.

It's worth examining this specific proposition in more detail by taking the opposite case: a thought experiment—imagine a world without institutions. And let us take a difficult context: the sometimes venal and secretive world of financial investment.

THE GIGANTIC PONZI SCHEME orchestrated by the financier Bernard Madoff was the world's largest fraud ever perpetrated by one man. It ruined thousands of investors and symbolized the most grotesque excesses of Wall Street. Despite the abject failure to catch Madoff by the government body established to police and regulate the investment industry, it was almost universally agreed that the best way to prevent such crimes in future was tighter regulation and scrutiny of the investment industry. The overwhelming reaction was that the government should have protected the innocent investors: Something must be done!

But there may be an alternative approach that overturns every assumption we have about how to deter, prevent and punish such crimes in future. It may be that the very rules and institutions established to protect us in fact do the opposite.

Madoff's fraud was simple. He encouraged investors to deposit money with his firm, paying them returns that were consistently higher than the going rate. With the appeal of above-market and above all steady returns, Madoff had little difficulty in attracting new investors. Their fresh deposits would be used to fund returns to the earlier investors. All the scheme required was a never-ending flow of new investors, with deposits sufficient to fund the above-market returns to the earlier investors, and to pay off the occasional depositor who wished to withdraw their whole investment—and for obvious reasons, those wishing to withdraw from this cash cow of easy money were few.

Madoff and his co-conspirators manufactured a huge volume of falsified reports and data to pretend that their fraudulent scheme was in fact a legitimate and highly successful investment business. Madoff's cover was effective. On three occasions in the 1990s, he was elected chairman of the NASDAQ. By his own admission, he perpetrated this massive fraud for nearly two decades, and was uncovered only when the precipitous market collapses at the end of 2008 prevented him from raising the funds to pay off those wishing to withdraw their money. In the end, it was estimated, Madoff's fraud cost his investors perhaps $20 billion.

Less simple is why a scheme of such magnitude and pervasive dishonesty succeeded for so long. Madoff lied systematically both to his investors and to the supervising federal authorities. In this criminal endeavor, he was apparently assisted by colleagues, some of whom have been prosecuted or face further investigation. But the scale of profits from his fund should have provoked more intrusive suspicion; few others within the industry tried to work out how his company could consistently make such high profits, against market trends, outperforming all competitors year after year.

The institutions designed to prevent such crime completely failed. The Securities and Exchange Commission, the federal body established in the 1930s to supervise the investment industry, conducted several investigations. Madoff himself has said that he had "hundreds" of contacts with SEC staff.[6] Prompted by tip-offs from others in the industry who questioned Madoff's fantastic profits, the SEC failed, however, to uncover the crime.

A later report on how the SEC missed Madoff found many failings: Staff were overspecialized, devoted to particular subsets of fraud and rewarded for pursuing that particular kind of crime.[7] Different parts of the SEC investigating Madoff were unaware of each other. Each individual part cleared Madoff of other allegations against him. Together, they managed to miss the big picture.

Elsewhere, the report revealed not only that SEC staff were often incompetent in understanding Ponzi schemes, but that Madoff intimidated SEC investigators because of his stature on Wall Street. The investigation at one point describes investigators as "enthralled" by Madoff: Some of them asked Madoff's staff if they could work for him.[8]

This failure appears part of a disquieting pattern. It was only *after* the BP Gulf oil spill of 2010 that the many failings of the body assigned to monitor and regulate the oil industry surfaced. In the aftermath of the disaster, it emerged that the Minerals Management Service (MMS) had allowed BP to skip environmental assessments ahead of drilling the well that spewed millions of barrels of oil into the Gulf. MMS inspectors had also permitted oil company employees to fill out inspection forms in pencil, which they would then ink in. Others had accepted illegal gifts, consumed drugs and literally gone to bed with officials from the companies they were supposed to regulate.[9] One inspector had negotiated a job with an oil company while at the same time inspecting the company's operations.

With Madoff, the financial industry's own self-regulatory bodies did nothing to investigate or stop his suspiciously profitable activities. This was unsurprising given that Madoff was a prominent member of many of them. Madoff was at various times chairman or board member of the National Association of Securities Dealers, a self-regulatory securities industry organization. The Madoff family had long-standing, high-level ties to the Securities Industry and Financial Markets Association, the primary securities industry organization. Madoff's brother Peter served two terms as a member of this organization's board of directors.

Madoff was regarded as a dominant figure in the investment industry, one of the largest "market makers" at the NASDAQ. He and his company were major political donors: Notably, he gave nearly a quarter of a million dollars to *both* Democrats and Republicans, indicative not of any political preference, but more a naked purchase of influence. Some have suggested that his political connections, and links to the SEC, helped deter a more thorough investigation of his activities.

The testimony of financial analyst and would-be Madoff whistle-blower Harry Markopolos to Congress, after the fraud was uncovered, was revealing. Giving evidence to the House of Representatives capital markets subcommittee, Markopolos said that he had investigated Madoff on behalf of a group of private investors.[10] After just a short examination of the numbers, he came to the conclusion that Madoff's spectacular returns could be explained by only one investment technique: fraud. Markopolos testified that for nine years he had repeatedly tried to get the SEC to investigate and shut down the Madoff Ponzi scheme. The SEC not only had ignored these warnings, according to Markopolos, but was fundamentally incapable of understanding the complex financial instruments being traded in the twenty-first century. And here lies one clue to what might be done to prevent such crime in future.

Another lies in an uncompromising look at the investors themselves. Many suffered terribly from Madoff's fraud, losing life savings, being forced to sell homes or return from a well-earned retirement to work indefinitely, their nest egg stolen. In many cases, their lives were utterly ruined. But why did these investors give their money to Madoff without the most cursory scrutiny of his company? Madoff's returns were so implausible that any sensible investor should have held back, but many committed their entire life savings. Harry Markopolos told Congress that investing in Madoff was a "no-brainer" in that "you had to have no brains whatsoever to invest into such an unbelievable performance record that bears no resemblance to any other investment manager's track record throughout recorded human history."

Some commentators have suggested that one of Madoff's techniques was to hint at a vague air of wrongdoing to help justify his otherwise inexplicable returns. The right to invest in his company was by invitation only, creating an air of desirable—and perhaps disreputable—exclusivity, that something special was going on, maybe something if not illegal then a little bit questionable: insider-trading perhaps, of some kind. For several years, potential investors who approached Madoff were told that the fund was "closed." Such false allure is the classic sign of a Ponzi scheme.

In *The New York Times*, business commentator Joe Nocera has argued that for these investors to blame the government for their decision to give every last penny to Bernie Madoff "is like a child blaming his mother for letting him start a fight while she wasn't looking."[11] But here lies one explanation of why people may have invested in Madoff. The mere existence of the SEC, with its claim to supervise, scrutinize and protect, must inevitably lower people's own sensitivity to risk. If the teacher is present, what is going on in the playground must be, in some way, acceptable.

Research suggests that when measures are in place to protect people from risk, they tend to indulge in *more* risky behavior. In his 2006 book *Government Failure Versus Market Failure*, Clifford Winston, an economist at the Brookings Institution, cites considerable and diverse research which shows, for instance, that people drive faster in vehicles that feel safer, cycle more dangerously when they wear helmets and take less care bathing infants when using child seats designed to reduce the risk of drowning.

This research makes sense. We tend to lower our guard when told that the coast is clear. Indeed, so evident is this fundamental human tendency that one can make a further, and perhaps provocative, presumption: that criminal frauds like Madoff's are actually made more feasible by the presence of institutional authorities designed to prevent them. The evidence for this seemingly outrageous claim is in front of our noses: The fraud happened, right under the SEC's nose.

Moreover, as the Madoff example has clearly shown, it is naive to expect any single authority to keep up with the massive complexity and dynamic changes of an industry like securities investment. There is a fundamental and insoluble imbalance in such supervision. Government bodies suffer the constant depredations of budget cycles, cuts and the intrinsic disadvantages of employers who can offer salaries equivalent to only a tiny proportion of those available in the industry they supervise. Given this fundamental and persistent power imbalance, it is surprising not that institutions like the SEC fail, as they regularly do, but that investors expect such institutions to keep up with the freewheeling, greed-tainted and secretive world of securities investment.

On the broader scale, it is often claimed that the recent global credit crisis was caused by the absence—or more precisely, the withdrawal—of the correct controls on the financial industry. It is persuasively argued that it was the proliferation of certain financial instruments, collectively known as derivatives, and specifically "credit default swaps" (or CDSs), which helped spread the poison of the subprime mortgage crisis across the world. CDSs are essentially legalized gambling: They are bets on whether certain financial indices, like mortgage repayments or stock prices, will rise or fall; a financial instrument that Warren Buffett has called "financial Weapons of Mass Destruction." Some have called them the twenty-first-century version of the 1920s "bucket shops," where people could bet on whether stocks would rise or fall without actually owning those stocks. The bucket shops were blamed for the wild speculation that helped fuel the Wall Street Crash of 1929. They were subsequently outlawed. In 2000,

Congress passed a little-known law that permitted such betting again. As for the industry's own alleged safeguards, banks *paid* the ratings agencies to rate and thus endorse the mortgage-based investment instruments that "sliced and diced" and concealed and spread the dangerous risk of subprime lending.

Many commentators have therefore reasonably concluded that the obvious answer is further regulation, to ban CDSs and rely on legislation to tame the industry. The problem with this analysis, however, so tempting in these turbid days, is that it rests on an assumption about the legislative process that is perilous indeed: that legislators act upon the interests of voters, and no one else. The law in question, the Commodity Futures Modernization Act, was passed in 2000 by a Democratic administration; it was proposed by the Clinton administration and passed quickly through both Houses. Not one member of Congress raised objections to this particular provision, which was secreted away in a bill of many hundreds of pages. Needless to say, that year the financial services industry, which strongly supported the bill, contributed large amounts to both Democrats and Republicans.

After the crash, politicians on both sides of the Atlantic roared their populist anger against the banks and mortgage companies that helped precipitate the crisis, then demanded massive government bailouts for their companies, while continuing to pay their executives grotesque bonuses. In all countries, political leaders queued up to decry the greed and swear their commitment to legislation that would "never again" allow such abuse to recur. But out of this bellowing public rage, what the legislation actually delivered resembled more a mouse's squeak.

The legislation is complex. In the U.S., the bill that finally passed in July 2010, allegedly to "reform Wall Street," is a document of thousands of pages.[12] Many of its provisions are highly technical in nature, allowing politicians to claim to an ill-informed public that the new law amounts to more than it in reality is. The press, in its complacency as the "fourth estate" in the body politic, did little to inquire into and explain the complexities. For instance, much was made of the prohibitions against "proprietary trading"; most people would have no clue what this actually is.

In fact, this prohibition, in any case very limited, will do almost nothing to prevent the kind of collapse that the global economy experienced in 2008 and 2009. Within months of the "reform Wall Street" legislation, banks were finding ways to circumvent this "Volcker rule" to limit trading—perhaps better known as betting—on their own accounts: precisely the activity that helped bring down Lehman Brothers in 2007.[13]

Most financial commentators agreed that there was one simple and easily explicable measure that would surely have limited the ability of banks to create the chaos that they did: limits on capital-to-loan ratios, i.e., require banks to hold more capital relative to their lending. In the confusion and obscurity of new measures, such rules were largely absent or, if present, in watered-down form. Instead, in a telltale signal that the necessary tough decisions had been dodged, Congress set up new bodies, and new mechanisms, to deal with these problems in the future. Likewise, amendments designed to address the problem of banks "too big to fail," by limiting their capital and thus the risk they pose to the whole economy, were rejected. Instead of passing the necessary measures in the immediate aftermath of the crash, when they might have been politically possible, the congressional legislation empowers a new regulatory body to pass them in future, when without doubt still less political support will be available. In a sure sign that the legislation was indeed to the benefit, not detriment, of the banks, shares in all financial service companies significantly rose immediately after the Senate vote.

Meanwhile, at the global level, neither the G20 nor the global banking regulatory mechanism, the Basel Committee, have managed to agree on measures to ensure that banks hold sufficient deposits against lending. The Basel III proposals in 2010, celebrated by the banking industry as a major step forward, were judged by a more independent and disinterested group of distinguished academic finance experts as "far from sufficient to protect the system from recurring crises."[14] Clive Crook in the *Financial Times* commented that the new Basel rules were an improvement on the preceding arrangements, but "not by much."[15]

The reason for this failure is not hard to find. As soon as anyone suggested more effective measures, like higher capital-to-lending ratios, legions of banking industry spokesmen would rise as one to complain that such requirements would render U.S. financial companies "uncompetitive" in the global market place. The CEO of JPMorgan Chase, for instance, wailed that new financial regulation including stricter capital controls would be the "nail in the coffin" of big American banks, adding for good measure that this would "greatly diminish growth."[16] This was a powerful argument in a country deeply mired in recession. But the argument rarely needed to be publicly advocated: There was precious little public debate on the bill, since politicians, both Democrats and Republicans, conspired to pretend that the bill had sharp teeth when in fact it was but a set of crummy plastic dentures.

This too was unsurprising, since the financial industry had taken care to donate generously to both sides. In advance of the congressional bill, financial institutions spent $1.4 million a day on lobbying; they had hired seventy former Congress members to their payroll, and 940 former federal employees. Senator Scott Brown, a Republican from Massachusetts, raked in "off-the-charts" donations from the financial industry while working to water down the financial bill.[17] On the Democrats' side, President Obama's then budget director, Peter Orszag, left the White House and waited a seemly four months before joining Citibank, which of course was busy marketing new credit cards to indebted Americans.

The congressional debate was in fact not a substantive discussion of what was really required to prevent another financial meltdown in the future. It was instead a kind of theatrical performance presented for the public's benefit to reassure them that "something was being done." The Republican chairman of the House Financial Services Committee, Spencer Bachus, soon afterward remarked with refreshing candor that "my view is that Washington . . . [is] there to serve the banks."

The answer then may be to do the one thing that no one seems prepared to contemplate: Take away the teacher in the playground. Let anarchy reign. It's interesting to contemplate what might follow. Some pointers are already available: in the behaviors and systems that have grown up on the World Wide Web.

On eBay and other online marketplaces, there are few certain methods to prevent fraud. It's easy for a seller to take payment online for imperfect or nonexistent products then disappear into the anonymous jungle of the Internet. When eBay began, the anonymity of the Web did little to produce trust. On the contrary, buyers and sellers were quick to complain about each other—often directly to Pierre Omidyar, the founder of eBay, who in the early days would answer customer service complaints himself. He was soon overwhelmed with the volume of complaints.

Omidyar decided to introduce a system under which eBay participants could rate each other online—not just to say when they were dissatisfied, but when they were happy, too. This feedback system is one of eBay's most well-known features: Sellers advertise their positive ratings as a selling point. Sellers without positive ratings struggle to find buyers. Thus, there is a huge incentive for sellers and buyers to treat each other well, if they are to do any repeat business. And interestingly, like the accumulation of friends on Facebook, which takes months and years to build up, the accumulation of trust indicators within this system is also a huge barrier to entry for prospective competitors to eBay.

The idea—and effect—was to incentivize sellers to behave well: to deliver what they sold promptly and in good order. The system seemed to work. Introduction of the ratings system helped drive a massive increase in transactions on eBay and a reduction in the number of fraud charges arising from eBay purchases.

In China, things have worked slightly differently, but prove the same point. Here, eBay lost market share to a competitor that understood better how customers wanted to build trust with one another. On its Chinese site, eBay did not offer ways for buyers and sellers to chat online, fearing they would close their transactions off the site to avoid paying fees. By contrast, eBay's rival service, Taobao.com, understood that live conversations were necessary for Chinese consumers to cultivate trust, and offered an instant-message service to allow them to haggle over deals. eBay forfeited the Chinese online market to Taobao partly as a result.

The online classifieds site Craigslist did something similar to eBay, following the philosophy of its founder, Craig Newmark, that "people are good and trustworthy and generally just concerned with getting through the day."[18] All you have to do is build a minimal infrastructure and let them work things out for themselves. The primary mechanism of the site is the red flag: If other users flag an unacceptable advertisement enough times, it will disappear. The mission of Craigslist is simple: to enable local, face-to-face transactions. This formula clearly works despite the many aesthetic flaws and frustrations of Craigslist. It is by far the most popular community site in the U.S., and is reportedly viewed by forty-seven million unique users each month.

The very openness of the Web, however, has brought to the surface some of mankind's worst aspects. But with the transparency, others are learning to combat the most undesirable and sometimes criminal activities.

For instance, in 2010, campaigners demanded that Craigslist remove its "Adult Services" section because it was being used by sex traffickers to pimp underage girls. Craigslist at first refused, citing its commitment to freedom of speech, but eventually succumbed to the pressure and removed the offending section. Likewise, Amazon removed a self-published book on pedophilia after mass Twitter and e-mail protests. In both cases, the action to address the offense took place with no government intervention.

Small businesses everywhere must rapidly adapt to a world where their services and products are discussed openly and critically on the Web by customers. Discomforting for some, the enforced visibility and criticism on the Web is proving for others a liberation, and a sales advantage. The evidence is mounting that, of two otherwise identical businesses, the one that responds quickly and positively and, above all, transparently to customer complaints online will rapidly gain the better online ratings, with positive consequences for its likely sales.

A new phenomenon is emerging on the Internet, which one commentator has called the "Panopticon."[19] The original Panopticon was an imaginary prison, designed by Jeremy Bentham, where all parts of the prison were visible from one central point, without the prisoners' knowing that they were under observation at any particular moment. But the Panopticon of the Internet is not for the observation by one of many, but more for "all watching all." As our lives are lived increasingly online, so are our traces apparent. More and more it is possible to locate, identify and examine people from their online presence.

There are obvious privacy concerns here, which we have yet properly to contend with. It is a new and disquieting world when a trainee teacher can be denied a college degree because she has posted a photo of herself, drunk, on Myspace.* But at the same time there is also the potential for a new form of collective security. Already, it is possible to easily access the human rights and environmental records of major companies;[20] one website allows you to research all the components, and the labor history embodied in them, of even complex products like computers or TVs.[21] It is easy to see how this scrutiny will spread more widely. Already, employers Google prospective employees to scrutinize their online history. Prospective lovers do the same. The Panopticon is already reality.

While online transparency and criticism may help improve the services offered by competing local plumbers, it's harder to see how they may work for the securities industry, a world that is not only secretive but also so complex that many of its most sophisticated

---

The New York Times reported that "Stacy Snyder, then a 25-year-old teacher in training at Conestoga Valley High School in Lancaster, Pa., posted a photo on her MySpace page that showed her at a party wearing a pirate hat and drinking from a plastic cup, with the caption 'Drunken Pirate.' After discovering the page, her supervisor at the high school told her the photo was 'unprofessional,' and the dean of Millersville University School of Education, where Snyder was enrolled, said she was promoting drinking in virtual view of her under-age students. As a result, days before Snyder's scheduled graduation, the university denied her a teaching degree." Jeffrey Rosen, "The Web Means the End of Forgetting," *The New York Times*, July 19, 2010.

denizens (George Soros, for instance) freely admit that they do not fully understand the financial instruments now available. Here, we return to Harry Markopolos.

After conducting his own investigation of Madoff, and concluding that something very fishy was going on, Markopolos sought to inform the SEC, which, as we now know, failed to follow up on his suspicions. This he was permitted to do by law. Markopolos was not, however, permitted to publicize his concerns, for to do so would have immediately made him vulnerable to punitive lawsuits by Madoff. Indeed, Markopolos testified that the failure of the SEC to investigate his complaints made him fear for his safety. The net effect, therefore, of the laws existing at the time of the Madoff fraud was not to inform and protect investors, but to protect Madoff.

Perhaps it is naive to expect ordinary investors to enjoy the expertise to scrutinize investment funds like Madoff's, even if one might expect them to exercise more diligence than that demonstrated by Madoff's unwise and unfortunate investors. It is not unrealistic, however, to envisage a system whereby disinterested experts might offer advice on the wisdom of investing in certain funds. Looking at the way e-commerce is developing on the Web, this might consist of several connected elements: a ratings system for buyers anonymously to rate their investment "experience," independent sites which offer disinterested advice on various investment alternatives and, finally, investors might form groups—like cooperatives—such as that which hired Harry Markopolos to conduct research on their behalf.

Above all, the Web shows that it is transparency that wins customers. Ergo, those that eschew it—or actively reject it, as Madoff did—should pay the penalty in lost business. Madoff himself has argued that his claimed "black box" investment strategy—the series of computerized algorithms to decide equity trades—was unintelligible to most of Wall Street, let alone ordinary investors, claiming that many other hedge funds are similarly opaque to outside scrutiny: "Does anyone know how, say, Renaissance really makes its returns?" Madoff asked in an interview with the *Financial Times*, referring to the wildly successful hedge fund.[22]

Perhaps he is right. However, what is beyond dispute is that from 1992 onward Madoff, by his own admission, conducted no trades at all and faked the documents, pretending that they had taken place. This fraud should have been easy to detect with only the most cursory scrutiny, if the market were more transparent: It should be straightforward to corroborate the trades with the counterparties, those who supposedly bought and sold Madoff's equity holdings. In other words, transparency does not need to reveal the secret investment strategies of successful funds, but it can—and simply—reveal other telltale signs of fraud like Madoff's. Unlike his faked investment strategy, Madoff's fraud was devastatingly simple.

There is perhaps a final and subtle lesson to be learned from this miserable episode. It is clear both from victims and Madoff himself that the wealth and power of big Wall Street players was a deterrent against scrutiny and investigation, intimidating those who sought to question, including the SEC. From many accounts of the Madoff scam, Wall Street appears as a layered hierarchy governed not by the SEC but by an exclusive club of powerful financiers, whom Madoff sought to join and succeeded in so doing. This club was bound by a wary but mutual trust and tacit agreement among members to forbear from questioning one another's affairs too closely. Madoff claims that many major Wall Street figures and banks, including JPMorgan, knew what was going on. Once Madoff joined the club, and hobnobbed with its members, he was all but untouchable.

We have been culturally conditioned to accept that the prosecution of the occasional Madoff somehow proves the power of law and intrinsic justice in the system. In fact, the story unearthed by his case proves the opposite: The system is revealed as fundamentally iniquitous and persistently vulnerable to crime and violent instability. The gross inequality of contemporary society permits a culture of unaccountability and, sometimes, criminality among the richest and most powerful. The most extreme results of this imbalance are scandals like Madoff, but also, with the credit crunch, economic volatility that destroys millions of jobs and endangers the entire global economy.

Methods to address this inequality will be discussed later. Money and power are of course hard to assail as sources of influence and secrecy. But what can be changed is the attitude of those outside the private circle. We should no longer be intimidated. One clear lesson of the Madoff scandal is the requirement for individual investors themselves to use greater care and scrutiny: to exercise, in short, their own agency rather than submitting their choices to the care of others. Everyone has the right to question. This is a right that cannot be taken for granted but that must be continually asserted, by one and by all. The more each of us demands it, the easier it will be for all of us.

The exercise of collective and individual scrutiny, disinterested analysis shared publicly, insistent questioning: None of these elements alone would necessarily suffice to deter or prevent future Madoffs. But together they would create a lattice of checks and balances whose collective effect would be to force greater transparency within, and scrutiny of, a notoriously closed, clubby and corrupt industry: a result that decades of government supervision and legislation have signally failed to achieve.

That lattice would not have a fixed structure, and it would likely change over time in response to changes in the industry it was monitoring. It would not have the reassuring bricks-and-mortar institutional presence, and claim to expertise and authority, of a body like the Securities and Exchange Commission—itself a comforting name, at least prior to Madoff. The lattice may not be imposed by legislation, and its origin may be in a state of affairs some might call anarchy—the absence of rules—but its result would be not the disorder usually associated with that word, but its opposite.

FOR TWO DAYS IN 2004, there was anarchy in Kosovo. The "authorities"—in this case the local police, UN and NATO peacekeepers—lost control. This was never publicly admitted. The candid admissions of failure in reports by UN officials in Kosovo itself were altered at UN headquarters in New York before they were reported to the UN Security Council, the ultimate authority which supervised the de facto government of Kosovo. It wasn't the UN's fault, the Security Council was told. The violence was deliberately instigated by extremist Kosovar leaders, an allegation for which there was little hard evidence.

The journalists who arrived in Kosovo after the violence chose their own convenient narratives: This was a typical, if depressing, cycle of the familiar ethnic violence that had plagued Kosovo, like the Balkans, for generations. Only a few chose to report the more complicated truth, including the fact that the violence had been in part a kind of rebellion against the ruling authorities in Kosovo—the UN. Only one NGO, a specialist in conflict whose two staff were deeply embedded in Kosovo's complicated stories, managed to capture the many strands of what had happened there.[23]

In truth, each chosen narrative carried some weight. The story of generational ethnic hatred was, in a sense, a true one. Serbs were attacked by Kosovo Albanian mobs across the territory; many Serbian houses were burned; some Serbs were physically assaulted; eight were killed (the remainder killed in the violence were Kosovo Albanians shot by NATO and UN forces).[24]

A second narrative was better concealed than the first, conventional account. This was that the anger was directed as much against the UN rulers of Kosovo as it was against the Serbs. Despite having their own democratically elected government, the people of Kosovo were excluded from the crucial decisions about their own future. I saw the evidence with my own eyes. The UN was attacked in all its manifestations—offices, cars, staff. Other international organizations, such as the EU, were not attacked.

There was a deeper flux at work too. The boys and young men in the rioting crowds were not sophisticated political critics. If you had asked them why they were rioting, they would not have said it was because Kosovo's people were excluded from political decision making about their future. They might have said, "We hate the Serbs." But what one most frequently heard was this: "It is because we are angry." Angry at the potholes and the lack of jobs; angry at the endless power cuts; angry because the girls and the luxury we see on MTV are unavailable to us.

So far, so political. But it was clear, because you could feel it, that there was a collective emotion at work. An emotion that was evident in individuals, but took greater force, and found expression, only when the crowd formed. The violence felt, in some terrible inadmissible way, like a release.

After the violence subsided, I returned to my work at the UN. My job had been to guide the local elected Kosovo government to adopt so-called standards of democracy: the rule of law, minority rights and other measures of a state's worthiness to exist and be accepted in the community of nations. The "international community" in this case was embodied in a small and secretive group of six countries known as the "Contact Group" which ran international policy on Kosovo. This group had insisted that such standards be established, and in some way fulfilled, before Kosovo could be considered for "final status"—whether it could become a state, as the large majority of its people desperately wanted.

Politically, the imposition of these standards was one reason why the violence had erupted. Because Russia, the U.S. and others disagreed in principle on whether Kosovo should become a state, no one in the "international community" was prepared to say *what* precisely Kosovo had to do to become independent. Kosovo was caught in a state of perpetual limbo, like being ordered every day to take an exam but never told if you'd passed or failed, or indeed what a pass or fail required.

The two-day orgy of violence, therefore, represented a total failure for my work. I sat at my desk, facing Besnik, my loyal assistant, and stared at the stacks of papers elaborating the democratic, rule-abiding "standards" that Kosovo was required to meet. We discussed whether to take the papers to the street outside the UN building, make a little pile and set fire to them. In the end we decided it would be a ridiculous and futile gesture: The rioters had already done it for us.

One incident, seemingly unremarkable, stuck in my memory. On the morning of the second day of the trouble, the head of the UN mission, a former president of Finland, had summoned Kosovo's political leaders to his office. He demanded to know what they were doing to stem the violence. As he read from a note prepared by his staffers, he looked over his spectacles at the leaders across the conference table, peering at them like a remonstrative schoolteacher at his unruly pupils.

And the leaders were silent. They sat glumly, looking a little shifty, like naughty schoolboys who had been caught smoking cigarettes behind the gym. A few of them muttered excuses, but those who did seemed as unconvinced as we were. There was a general air of embarrassment.

I pondered this incident. Why had the leaders not spoken up for their political demands? Why had they not blamed the UN and the international community for stoking the frustrated anger of the Kosovo Albanian majority? Why had they resembled nothing so much as a bunch of adolescents being punished after school?

Slowly, it dawned on me. No one was prepared to take responsibility for the violence, because no one *felt* responsible for it. The behavior of Kosovo's leaders was immature and childish, because that was what was expected of them. The international community had refused to give these political leaders the real responsibility to run the country, telling them instead that they and their country were not yet ready for the burdens of statehood. My work in elaborating and implementing the "standards" sent, and made concrete, this very message.

Kosovo was permitted to have elections, an elected government and a parliament, but the real power resided in an unelected official— the UN Special Representative, the former Finnish president, who was appointed by the UN Secretary-General—who could veto any decision made by the local elected government.

The dramatic events in one small Balkan province (now a state) were unique, but there are nevertheless lessons of broader significance.[25] Western democracies are not on the cusp of violent disorder (although it cannot be ruled out if the current system is not improved). The violence and unrest on the streets of Kosovo, but above all the feckless behavior of Kosovo's elected but powerless politicians, carried one crucial lesson: If people do not have responsibility, do not expect them to behave responsibly.

This episode suggests a broader lesson about democracy, stability and anarchy. Defenders of the current order argue that to abandon the system of representative democracy is to invite anarchy, a war of all against all. But the 2004 disorder in Kosovo suggests a more subtle and unexpected lesson. It is this: The *less* people have agency—control—over their own affairs, and the less command they feel over their futures and their circumstances, the *more* inclined they are to take to the streets. The best way, indeed, to invite violent anarchy is to *reduce* the agency and sense of control that people need to feel over their lives.

The disconnection between voters and their government, along with government's declining ability to deal with problems of global origin, are combining in the current dispensation to produce this very effect. The frustration, disillusionment and growing extremism all too evident in today's democracies are symptoms of this phenomenon: loss of agency. Kosovo may represent an extreme case, but for it not to become a harbinger, action must be taken. Our way of doing politics, indeed our way of thinking about politics, needs to change, from passivity to action: reclaiming agency.

And in that reclamation, we must find better ways of doing business with one another. If too distant and corruptible institutions are proving inadequate, what might work? Some believe that technology alone, and the Internet in particular, can deliver the necessary revolution. Some even believe that the Internet *is* the necessary revolution, and that its inherently heterogeneous and transparent nature amounts, in itself, to political change. Closer analysis reveals, however, a more complicated and ambiguous reality.

Something else is needed. And that something else, it turns out, doesn't require fancy technology, Web-based platforms and Twitter feeds (though they may help). That something else turns out to be simple indeed.

4

THE IMPORTANCE
OF MEETING PEOPLE

During the Spanish Civil War, more than thirty thousand people from over fifty nations volunteered to fight the Nationalist armies of General Franco. Many gave up jobs and left families in order to fight the emerging global threat of fascism, and to defend a nascent socialist, even anarchist republic.

They joined Republican forces that were in many cases undertrained and equipped with antique and inadequate weapons. In *Homage to Catalonia*, George Orwell vividly describes the miserable conditions of the front-line troops, dug into feces-strewn trenches with neither the clothing nor the arms needed to properly fight Franco's armies, which by contrast received substantial international support from Italy and Nazi Germany.* Yet Orwell compellingly evokes

---

*An international embargo was in theory supposed to stop arms supplies to both sides, but its enthusiastic enforcement by Britain, France and others had the principal effect of denying arms

the comradeship among the Republican troops, the abolition of traditional hierarchies and the appealing idealism of both the Spanish and international volunteers. He recounts too that anarchist principles were no obstacle to effective military organization: Although there was debate within army units—and a welcome absence of the cringing deference of many military organizations—there was also discipline, not least thanks to the unity of purpose among the troops.

Much history since has given the impression that the international volunteers were mainly middle-class intellectuals. But in fact they came from all walks of life.[1] The "International Brigade" of foreign volunteers fought in several key battles of the Civil War, including a notable role in the ferocious Battle of Madrid, where Republican forces successfully beat back a Nationalist assault in the autumn of 1936. The fighting was intense and bloody: Infantry fought at close quarters, room by room, with bayonets and grenades.

Of the thirty thousand or so foreign volunteers who went to fight for their beliefs, nearly ten thousand were killed in action and another eight thousand or so were wounded. Of those who survived, many returned to a less than welcoming reception in their home countries. Some were imprisoned, others were denied citizenship, while some, such as the three thousand or so antifascist Germans, were unable to return home at all.

---

to the Republicans. Nazi Germany and Mussolini's Italy, meanwhile, breached the embargo to support the Francoists with impunity. A similar situation arose during the breakup of Yugoslavia in the 1990s, when a UN arms embargo, proposed and enforced by the UK, U.S. and others, failed to diminish the military effectiveness of the genocidal armies of the Bosnian Serbs (mainly because they already enjoyed the considerable military resources of the former Yugoslav army). The UN embargo, however, considerably hindered the defenses of their victims, the Bosnian Muslims and Croats. The effect of that embargo therefore, as with Spain in the 1930s, was to deliver a military advantage to the fascist aggressor. In the 1930s, this was indeed the intent.

THE LEADERLESS REVOLUTION

THE WAR IN THE DARFUR REGION of Sudan has been raging since 2003. Civilian casualties are enormous, with some estimating that several hundred thousand people have been killed, and perhaps three million refugees displaced. The killing has been sustained and deliberate, leading many to depict the conflict as a planned genocide of the indigenous inhabitants of Darfur, engineered and led by the Sudanese government in Khartoum and executed by militias under its control, including the notorious Janjaweed. In 2008, the president of Sudan, Omar Hassan al-Bashir, was indicted for war crimes by the International Criminal Court in The Hague. At the time of this writing, however, Bashir has not been handed over to the court for trial;* all the signs indicate that the "international community," including the U.S., is prepared to allow the indictments to be quietly forgotten.

But nongovernmental reaction to the killings in Darfur has been vociferous. Across the world, hundreds of protest groups have demanded action to stop the killing, calling for the intervention of foreign troops either under United Nations or African Union auspices. Some protest groups, such as Not on Our Watch, were set up by famous film stars, including George Clooney and Brad Pitt.[2] Students from Swarthmore College set up a telephone hotline that immediately connects callers to the office of their representative in Congress, whom they can tell to take action about Darfur. There have been a large number of Internet petitions about Darfur, some attracting many millions of signatories.

But this vast expenditure of campaigning energy has resulted in scant additional protection for Darfuri civilians. As the war raged,

---

*In its first ten years of operation, the court has failed to secure any convictions.

the "international community's" response amounted to a small and underequipped African Union force, which, several years after the conflict began, could offer only a few thousand lightly armed troops to provide security in an area approximately the size of Spain. Even the force's defenders make no claim that the AU force is in any way adequate to deter or prevent attacks against civilians. And indeed, the killing has continued up to the time of this writing.

Some commentators have suggested that the rhetorical heat generated by Western pressure groups, and in particular their use of the word "genocide," may have made the chances of finding a peaceful outcome locally more difficult.[3] Just as distant governments must simplify the complex realities of foreign conflicts in order to pronounce policy about them, so too did the simplifying lens of distance enable campaigners to turn a complicated and fluid situation into a compelling black-and-white narrative of good and evil, leading some to argue that the simplifications of celebrity campaigning have actually helped prolong the conflict.[4] No foreign citizen has taken up arms themselves to defend the Darfuris.

THE ADVENT OF THE INTERNET has released a wave of enthusiasts who believe that democracy can be improved—saved, perhaps—by technology alone. There are now innumerable websites where online petitions can be created and propagated on any topic, from freeing imprisoned Burmese democracy leader Aung San Suu Kyi to liberating socialite Paris Hilton from her brief incarceration for drunk driving. Politicians have been quick to glom on to the petition trend. The website of the British prime minister, like that of the White House, encourages their submission, though there is little mention of what becomes of any petition thus delivered. The woefully undemocratic British House of Lords, where every member is either appointed or inherits his seat, recently established an equally pitiful blog site to encourage "dialogue" between Their Lordships and the grateful public.[5] Even the British sovereign, to whom all Britons are subject, now has a Facebook page where the Queen's subjects can ventilate their feelings.

Not one to miss out on a trend, China's Communist Party, a body not best known for accountability and transparency, has launched its own discussion forum, "Direct line to Zhongnanhai." Zhongnanhai is the huge and secretive compound in the heart of Beijing where China's leaders live and work. As one commentator aptly put it, "The site appears to be an effort to persuade people that the leadership is listening to their very personal concerns. . . . It is clearly designed to demonstrate that the leadership is attentive and sensitive."[6] But as the *Financial Times* reported, although the new message board is trying to demonstrate responsiveness, it does not actually provide responses from the leaders addressed. A further problem with "Internet democracy" was revealed when such an attempt was mounted during the transition period after the U.S. presidential election of 2008. When the new administration of President-elect Barack Obama created an online "Citizen's Briefing Book" for people to submit ideas "virtually" to the president, they received over forty thousand proposals and nearly a million and a half people voted on their preferences among those proposals. The most popular idea was to legalize marijuana. Legalizing online poker topped the contributions in the technology category. Revoking the Church of Scientology's tax-exempt status garnered three times more votes than raising funds for childhood cancer. *The New York Times'* conclusion from this episode was that advocates of the Internet as the incarnation of real-time participatory democracy—"Athens on the Net"—still had some arguments to answer.[7]

There are now websites that invite views on proposed legislation, scrutiny of campaign finances and details of your representatives' voting patterns. "See, click, fix" allows citizens to identify local problems online for government action.[8] But all these supposedly new forms of political action rely on a very traditional mechanism of political change—*up/down*: pressuring, scrutinizing, demanding that representatives and government take action. There has been no change to the fundamental model of politics.

It is correspondingly easy for government and other embodiments of the status quo to adopt these new technological tools, and thus neutralize any benefit. Governments are now replete with their own tech fetishists, wittering on (or twittering on) about "Government 2.0" and organizing podcasts, tweets and blogs saying more or less the same things that politicians have always said, albeit through a different medium.

Despite the repeated claim from government that the flow of information is from people to government, the evidence suggests that the true direction is the opposite. There is scant evidence to suggest that any significant government policy has been informed or altered by tweeting or the fancy online tools set up, for instance, by the U.S. State Department to encourage a "global conversation." The basic power structure is unchanged—up/down—the only difference is the *form* of communication. Revealingly, the most palpable results of this "new" Web activism are to be found in the most traditional manifestations of "old" politics: organizing get-out-the-vote volunteers and, inevitably, raising money.

Celebrants of the new technological democracy often cite examples from "abroad" where technology has brought about political change, like the "color revolutions" in Ukraine or Georgia, or the "Twitter protests" against the government in Iran in 2009, and most recently the revolutions in Tunisia and Egypt in the "Arab spring" of 2011, where indeed it is clear that social media played an important role.

They rarely mention that there are equally many examples where technology has had a more malign effect. In Nigeria, deadly riots in the city of Jos were fueled, according to one authority, by text messages sent between rampaging mobs;[9] the same thing happened in the violence that gripped Kosovo in 2004 (described in the previous chapter). In London, the killing of a fifteen-year-old boy was coordinated by his attackers on Facebook.* The "Twitter protests" in Iran did not lead, yet, to the overthrow of government; many protesters ended up in the same prison very traditionally used by different regimes to house political prisoners—Tehran's notorious Evin jail. These prisoners now include Iran's best-known blogger, Hossein Derakhshan, who in 2010 was sentenced to nineteen years in jail for alleged collaboration with foreign governments, spreading "propaganda" against the Islamic regime and setting up "obscene" websites.

In early 2011, the dictatorial regime in Sudan learned quickly from the Mubarak regime's mistakes in managing Internet-based protest in Egypt. Khartoum turned the Internet against the protesters, setting up fake pro-democracy pages on Facebook and arresting all those who showed up for the demonstrations advertised on the site. Eventually, activists avoided using Internet-based tools at all, returning to

---

*In U.S. prisons, the proliferation of smart phones has allowed incarcerated criminals to keep organizing drug and gang activity outside; Facebook, Twitter and e-mail lists were used to coordinate recent protests in several prisons. See Kim Severson and Robbie Brown, "Outlawed, Cellphones Are Thriving in Prisons," *The New York Times*, January 2, 2011.

more traditional and covert forms of organization.[10] The lesson is stark: Power adapts to new technology, and swiftly.

After an initial spasm of excitement at the liberating possibilities of the World Wide Web, it is now emerging that China's adoption of the Internet does not necessarily herald a new dawn of transparency and incipient democracy. Every major Internet company in China employs scores and sometimes hundreds of Internet "administrators" to search for subversive content. The city of Beijing recently advertised for ten thousand volunteers to act as monitors.[11] Twitter, Facebook and YouTube remain blocked. China is adapting search technology similar to Google's to hunt and prosecute dissent. The search company that pioneered the antidissident algorithms is now a successful commercial company, which is listed on the Chinese stock exchange—a neat rebuttal of the naive equation that free markets ipso facto produce freedom of speech.

In general, the protection of basic freedoms on the Web relies on the goodwill and good intentions of the very small number of people who control its most powerful institutions: the very opposite of the ideal condition required for the maintenance of freedom and democracy. Large companies—Yahoo!, AOL, Google—dominate decisions about what content may appear on the Web; one can only hope they are beneficent. Google alone controls 63 percent of Internet searches. In deciding what can or cannot be published on the Web and listed in its searches, and whether to comply with censoring governments, Google is taking decisions of immense consequence for freedom of speech. Its decision to confront censorship in China in early 2010 was a decision of great political, and not merely commercial, consequence.

As Google stood up to China, Microsoft without apology continued to offer a censored search service. Yahoo! and Microsoft have been accused by Amnesty International of abetting censorship and repression in China by supplying equipment and adapting their search engines to block certain sites and, in Yahoo!'s case, assisting the Chinese authorities in identifying online antigovernment critics. In response, they have argued that no company alone can change Chinese law, by which they must abide.

Eli Pariser of MoveOn has warned of a more subtle danger: that Google and Facebook's filtering mechanisms are creating a "filter bubble" around us; the algorithms applied by these sites to "personalize" our Web experience are effectively rendering much of the Web invisible.[12] We think we are browsing the entire World Wide Web, but in fact we are seeing only the sites Google and Facebook's filters deem appropriate to our interests. The Web surfer in China experiences the same phenomenon. There is no outward sign that the sites they are visiting have been vetted—or filtered—for their consumption by the sophisticated filtering technology used by the Chinese government. Unwitting, they think that they are surfing the whole Web. In this regard, they are just like Web users in the West.

As Stanford University's Professor Lawrence Lessig has argued, it is hard always to square the interests of a commercial company seeking to expand market share with the protection of freedom of speech: "[Google has] enormous control over a platform of all the world's data, and everything they do is designed to improve their control of the underlying data. If your whole game is to increase market share, it's hard to do good, and to gather data in ways that don't raise privacy concerns or that might help repressive governments to block controversial content."[13]

At least the Internet, it is argued, will encourage debate and interaction, albeit virtually rather than in person. But here, it appears that instead of encouraging debate among those of differing views and thus convergence, the opposite may be happening. The Web offers multiple locations to find those one agrees with, and to avoid those one doesn't. As columnist Nicholas Kristof has commented, we select the kind of news and opinions that reflect our own prejudices back to us, an emerging news product Nicholas Negroponte of MIT has called "The Daily Me."[14]

One result is that any clash of opinions, especially in the anything-goes anonymity of the Web, is increasingly violent, hostile and insulting. Name-calling is frequent; reasoned debate rare. Particularly when opinions differ from the party line—whether of left or right—criticism tends to escalate, and coarsen. It's not only domestic debates that witness such growing vituperation. In China, when a Chinese fighter plane crashed after colliding with a U.S. reconnaissance aircraft over the South China Sea, and its pilot died, the Chinese blogosphere erupted with violently anti-American and nationalist sentiment—views that the Chinese government was happy, at least at first, to allow, perhaps as a means to ventilate more general political frustrations. Demonstrations followed, and the American embassy in Beijing was attacked by stone-throwing hordes. Some demanded that China declare war on the U.S. The traditional state-controlled press, while critical of the U.S., had taken a more measured tone. The Chinese authorities struggled to contain the situation and began to downplay the issue in public. Some of the more rabid blogs were closed down. Eventually, the riots stopped. Back in the U.S., the government's director of National Intelligence has observed that the Internet is a fertile breeding ground for terrorism, warning that "when it comes to susceptibility to radicalization, virtual communities have become as important as physical communities."[15]

The antagonism and hostility of political debate on the Internet reveals an essential truth of the modern condition, which is in fact a perpetual condition of humanity, but one that modernity places in starker relief: The more detached people are from one another, the more they can cloak themselves in anonymity and be shielded from the consequences of their views, the more violent, hostile and irresponsible they are likely to be. It is a peculiar but retrograde feature of modernity that its facets—the nature of modern work, communications, political interaction and the modern state itself—have heightened that detachment.

There is a form of politics which produces more consensus, a better understanding and respect for alternative points of view and a deeper acknowledgment of facts over opinion. It does not require an expensive computer or any technical equipment at all, for the Internet often excludes the poor and otherwise marginalized.* It is as old-fashioned as the earliest parliaments, where people gathered on a hillside to arbitrate their common business. The academic who has pioneered the technique calls it "deliberative democracy," but really it can be called something simpler: meeting people.

AFTER HURRICANE KATRINA, much of the infrastructure of New Orleans was devastated: More than 70 percent of housing was damaged and entire neighborhoods were almost completely destroyed; schools, hospitals and police stations were shut down. Nearly a hundred thousand jobs were lost, and eighteen months after the hurricane, more than half of the city's population had not returned.

In the aftermath, plans to rebuild New Orleans confronted a ravaged infrastructure, enormous financial losses, a local government in disarray and a citizenry whose trust in government had been sorely undermined. The early planning efforts by city officials were met with

---

*The so-called digital divide.

anger and protest as the community struggled with the challenges of distributing resources and reviving an entire city.

Faced with this crisis of confidence, city officials decided to involve the citizens in a full discussion, in depth and face-to-face, on the priorities for the city. Most of the city's inhabitants were still spread across the U.S., not yet able to return. Four thousand New Orleanians met in "Community Congresses" staged across the country to discuss recovery priorities for their city. As decision makers listened, citizens discussed how to ensure safety from future flooding, empower residents to rebuild safe and stable neighborhoods, provide incentives and housing so people could return, and establish sustainable and equitable public services.[16]

At the end of the deliberations, fully 92 percent of participants agreed on the "Unified Plan" for the city. Critically, this approval rating represented the collective view of the citizenry: Participants reflected pre-Katrina New Orleans—in proportion to both race and income. At earlier similar events, black and poor citizens were often severely underrepresented. This time, citizens had participated not only at home but in cities across the country where hurricane refugees were then living. Thus, the city's new plan was discussed and endorsed not just by its officials, but also by its citizens, who overwhelmingly committed to support the plan.

There has been a more sustained experiment in such "participative" or "deliberative" democracy in Porto Alegre, one of Brazil's largest cities. "The Porto Alegre Experiment" again shows that better outcomes result when citizens are directly involved in decisions over their own lives. In 1989, when the experiment began, the city suffered some of the worst inequality in the continent. The poor—one-third of the city's population—lived in slums around the periphery; the rich controlled the city's government and budget. Over the last ten years, the city has gradually developed a multilayered approach to participatory budgeting. Starting at the most local level, citizens are encouraged to participate in debates about local spending priorities—water, schools, hospitals, housing, roads. Of the city's 1.5 million inhabitants, every citizen is informed about the budget process and around fifty thousand now take part.

According to a World Bank study, the participatory process has fostered direct improvements in facilities in Porto Alegre. For example, sewer and water connections increased from 75 percent of households in 1988 to 98 percent in 1997. The number of schools has increased fourfold since 1986. The city is at the cutting edge in developing progressive recycling and renewable energy projects. The participatory process is overwhelmingly supported by the city's population. It has also, reportedly, encouraged a change in the tenor of local politics. Less and less a partisan contest, the common enemy is the occasional crisis. Everything is transparent, from decision making to the awarding of contracts.

These new deliberative processes are locally driven and designed for local circumstances; there is no "One size fits all." The general benefits—of greater citizen empowerment, of greater consensus over local spending—are clear: They flow directly and crucially from the *agency* of those involved. People participate not to be consulted by government and service providers but to make real decisions themselves about their circumstances. And when people are trusted and informed to make decisions, they tend to make good ones. Such deliberative processes, with real decisions as their result, are not to be confused with America's overheated "town hall" meetings of recent memory, or the vulgar arguments on Internet "forums." While politicians claim they are intended as a place to hear the views of the public, town hall meetings are not places where decisions are made.

Typically, the local angry brigades line up to denounce elected officials and their plans, providing an unpleasant experience for everyone except those who enjoy public confrontation. Rational discussion and respect for the facts are, unsurprisingly, rarely the result.

In a recent book, legal scholar Cass Sunstein has noted that very often when groups of people are placed together to debate an issue, they often end up more polarized than at the beginning.[17] But Sunstein's work also suggests how to create greater unity. The more detached groups are from society, the more extreme their decisions are likely to become. The less that a decision debated within a group actually *matters*, the greater the likelihood of dispute and conflict. A lesson becomes clear: When nothing is at stake, and when no one has agency, it is predictable that heated disagreement will be the outcome.

It is not only hurricane-struck New Orleans that suffers a crisis in democracy. With turnouts falling and disaffection with "politics" growing in all democratic countries, its model, like that of Porto Alegre, offers lessons applicable beyond the occasional management of disasters.

One particular example of that crisis is found at the European Parliament. Originally conceived and empowered to give European peoples a voice in EU decisions largely dominated by governments, its problems highlight weaknesses increasingly apparent in other democratic legislatures.

At the most recent elections to the parliament, extremist parties jumped at the opportunity offered by the dismal turnout of Europe's voters—the lowest in the parliament's history. Realizing that many mainstream voters would stay away, extreme and far-right parties made special efforts to mobilize their supporters. The result was that such parties were represented in greater number here than in their own national parliaments. The right-wing British National Party joined Italian and Lithuanian proto-fascists, Dutch anti-immigrant parties and other assorted representatives of the fringe in the home of European "democracy."

Neither phenomenon—low turnout, extreme political parties— bodes well for the legitimacy, popularity or effectiveness of the decisions arising from the parliament. Both phenomena, however, point to a future of democratic politics, of both disenchantment and extremism, that may become more and more evident, in more established parliaments and congresses too. What is to be done?

The *Financial Times* recently reported an exercise which sought to address this problem, asking the question: How much longer can the EU continue as a project controlled by elites and disregarded by the masses?[18] What is the solution to this "democratic deficit"?

One answer was attempted by Professor James Fishkin, a social scientist at Stanford University. He conducted an experiment in which a balanced sample of 348 Europeans from the EU's twenty-seven countries were brought to Brussels for a three-day dialogue on the elections and the policy issues surrounding them. This is a procedure known as "deliberative polling," a concept Professor Fishkin introduced in 1988.

One outcome of the exercise was that many participants changed their voting intentions as a result of the dialogue. Beforehand, 40 percent said they would vote for mainstream center-right parties, 22 percent for socialists, 9 percent for centrist liberals and 8 percent for Greens. After the exercise, support for the center-right dropped to 30 percent, socialists and liberals were almost unchanged at 21 percent and 8 percent, respectively, and the Greens shot up to 18 percent.

Deliberative Democracy

CARNE ROSS

The rise in support for the Greens came about as a result of detailed discussions among the participants on climate change. Participants were asked to choose between the view that "we should do everything possible to combat climate change even if that hurts the economy" and the alternative view that "we should do everything possible to maximize economic growth, even if that hurts efforts to combat climate change." Before the discussions, 49 percent wanted to emphasize the fight against climate change. Afterward, this figure rose to 61 percent.

Exercises like that performed by Professor Fishkin, and the New Orleans reconstruction plan too, have shown repeatedly that when a group of people gathers together to consider their affairs and collective response to them—and, crucially, make decisions—a number of valuable benefits follow:

1. Participants pay greater heed to each other's positions and are more likely to acknowledge the concerns that underlie other people's political views.
2. There is a deeper consideration of facts—including scientific data—than normal political debate, composed largely of opinions, allows.
3. Partly as result of numbers 1 and 2, such exercises usually produce a greater degree of consensus within the group.
4. The group feels a much greater commitment to decisions reached collectively in this manner than to decisions imposed by any other authority.

Fishkin calls this "deliberative democracy." It is a process of a different order from the current system, prevalent in all democratic states, of *representative* democracy, whereby citizens elect representatives to make decisions on their behalf. Indeed, deliberative democracy in its fullest form, where people make genuine decisions of consequence as a group, or a grassroots, community-based democracy, is in fact ultimately incompatible with representative democracy. If two mechanisms make decisions, what if their choices are contradictory? One must be supreme.

Professor Fishkin attempts to bridge this problem, and render deliberative techniques compatible, by proposing that deliberative *polling*, of the kind described above, should help inform the regular structures of representative democracy—the legislators and members of the executive who make up the decision makers. But despite his efforts to construct such groups as representative of the general populace—by selecting their members in proportion to the political support for different parties in the broader population—such "deliberative polling" groups fail in one fundamental regard: They lack legitimacy. They are not elected, so why should their voice, however proportionately it might represent the rest, be heard above others?

Polling—like frequent referendums—fails in another regard too. While polls may provide an indication of what people think on a particular question at a particular moment, they leave out one crucial component of Fishkin's experiments—the *deliberation*: the talking, the to-and-fro, the listening, the compromise. Any citizen of California, where referendums are frequent, will recognize that they have done little to contribute to responsible and effective government of the state—rather the opposite. This is also why Internet surveys of opinion, or petitions, tend to the extreme, and are so pathetically inadequate as a new form of democracy.

In his essay "The Pursuit of the Ideal," Isaiah Berlin concludes that in deciding what to do, the only option, in private life as in public policy, is to engage in trade-offs—rules, values, principles must yield to each other in varying degrees in specific situations, adding that "a certain humility in these matters is very necessary" since we have no guarantee that any particular course we choose will be right. This is the essence of democracy: discussion of differing views and options on how we together must live, with a view—ultimately—to collective decision. The mere ventilation of opinions, whether in person or online, does not qualify.

In microcosm, it is self-evident that encounters and negotiation offer a greater possibility for respect and agreement than either the virtual chat room or a distant authority. Difficult discussions with friends or family can quickly degenerate online as misunderstandings; willful misinterpretations multiply. No one pretends that meetings in person are necessarily easier, or less painful, but somehow we are able to see and feel more and thus achieve a greater comprehension. Perhaps, above all, we simply spend more time.

Professor Fishkin's excellent books are filled with examples of deliberative democracy, and his comprehensive analysis of why and how it works and the impressive results it clearly delivers. But by and large, deliberative democracy has remained a matter for academic discussion, and occasional illustrative, yet tantalizing, exercises of the kind that took place in New Orleans or Porto Alegre, or the experiments practiced by Professor Fishkin.

The trouble with deliberative democracy is, of course, that it poses a direct challenge to the existing constitutional order of representative democracy, where the few are elected to arbitrate the affairs of the many. Deliberative polling, while imaginative and revealing in its insights, fails to bridge the gap. For in the existing system, it is not tolerable to the existing authority for citizens to gather to sort out their affairs and make decisions with real effects. That is what governments are for!

For deliberative decision making to function properly, and for citizens to enjoy its full and evident benefits, a condition must apply which, oddly, even the most ardent academic proponents of deliberative techniques seem loath to confess: There must be no other authority, *at all*.

THOUGH IT IS RARELY MENTIONED, even in the histories of that period, the Spanish Civil War saw a moment, tragically brief, of real existing anarchism. In the area of Spain under Republican control, anarchists for a short while held sway, as far as that term means anything when no one was completely in charge. This was not anarchy, an absence of order, it was a society that for a period decided to govern itself not by centralized authority, but by the wishes of local communities, workers, men and women, led by values of equality and mutual respect.

This happened between 1936 and 1938, and was confined mostly to parts of Catalonia in northern Spain, including Catalonia's capital, Barcelona. It was estimated that perhaps ten million people participated in this "Spanish Revolution" where farms and factories, and even shops and barbers, were collectivized and run along communal lines—neither owned by the state nor private capital, but run by the peasants and workers themselves. Decisions were made on libertarian principles—by those affected, without bureaucracy. In many areas, agricultural production significantly increased.

By 1938, it was over. The Communist Party in Moscow decided that Spain was not ready for proletarian revolution—at least not this kind—and ordered its cohorts in Spain, the local Communists, to suppress the anarchists. There were mass arrests, street fighting and executions. Anarchist leaders and parties were denounced. This repression was one of the reasons for the ultimate defeat of the Republicans, and the ensuing four decades of fascist dictatorship under Franco.

George Orwell's memoir of his experience in Catalonia contains vivid depictions of what anarchism, in practice, was really like. When published, *Homage to Catalonia* was attacked in Britain and elsewhere, above all by Communists and the left in general, who rejected its account of Communist suppression of the anarchists, preferring Moscow's propaganda that the anarchists were somehow in Franco's pay or otherwise to blame for the in-fighting in the antifascist ranks.

Homage sold very few copies on initial publication. Even now, the book is rarely seen for what it truly is, and is instead interpreted as a tragic and picturesque account of failed resistance against fascism.[19] Orwell had joined a small Marxist-oriented party, POUM,* in order to fight fascism, but later in the book confesses that if he had the choice again, he would have been an anarchist. He describes life in Barcelona during anarchism:

> Many of the normal motives of civilized life—snobbishness, money-grubbing, fear of the boss, etc.—had simply ceased to exist. The ordinary class division of society had disappeared to an extent that is almost unthinkable in the money-tainted air of England; there was no one there except the peasants and ourselves, and no one owned anyone else as his master. Of course such a state of affairs could not last. It was simply a temporary and local phase in an enormous game that is being played out over the whole surface of the Earth. But it lasted long enough to have its effect upon anyone who experienced it. However much one cursed at the time, one realized afterwards

---

*Partido Obrero de Unificación Marxista, or Workers' Party of Marxist Unification.

that one had been in contact with something strange and valuable. One had been in a community where hope was more normal than apathy or cynicism, where the word "comrade" stood for comrade-ship and not, as in most countries, for humbug. One had breathed the air of equality.[20]

This description tantalizes with its suggestion of what might be possible if self-organized government were to become reality. *Homage to Catalonia* also tells a vivid story about how one generation chose very directly to tackle the problems of the world, in this case fascism. And it is to this global stage that we must now turn. For here particularly, perhaps even more than in the domestic realm, governments and their organizations claim to have matters in hand. And in general, it seems, we are happy to believe them. On the world stage, in general, the management of "international affairs" is left to practitioners like statesmen and diplomats, which I once was.

It seems at first sight a reasonable bargain. The world is complicated; it requires professionals to sort it out. But as we shall see in later chapters, the bargain, like the pact between government and voter at home, seems to be breaking down. Established systems of interstate cooperation do not seem to be producing the solutions the world needs. But there is a worse and more pernicious effect too.

Somewhere along the way, it has become accepted that in representing a state, normal moral rules are suspended. Under the catch-all moral permission of *droit d'état*, officials acting in the name of the state, even law-abiding democracies like Britain or the U.S., are entitled to forsake normal moral inhibitions, like those against killing or causing harm to others. If such actions are justified by the needs of the state, not only are they excused, they are explicitly available. Indeed, the good diplomat is told to reject the softheaded morality of ordinary people if he is to practice his trade as it must be practiced—realpolitik. If death and the suffering of others are the result, this is a necessary price of protecting our own.

I have not come by this criticism by way of academic study or historical research. I know this because once I did it. I helped do harm to innocent others, with the explicit moral cover of the state, safe in the knowledge that I would never be held to account. With the comfort of impunity, I once committed violence in the name of the state.

5

THE MAN IN
THE WHITE COAT

The experiment conducted in the early 1960s by the Yale psychologist Stanley Milgram is a well-known demonstration of how authority can incite people to undertake heinous acts. Conducted soon after the 1961 trial of the Nazi Adolf Eichmann, Milgram's experiment showed how otherwise normal individuals could be instructed to commit horrific acts, including torture and murder, if commanded to do so by a person of sufficient, even if feigned, authority.

But the experiment also illustrates a problem that pervades the current international system and the current practice of diplomacy. That problem has a name—amorality: the profoundly negative moral consequences of officials, in this case diplomats, of not taking responsibility for what they do. And as we shall see, not only is it a problem of diplomacy, it is a problem of any system that suppresses people's sense of agency.

Milgram arranged a fake experiment whereby volunteers were instructed to give ever greater electric shocks to another participant in the experiment, unknown to the volunteer, an actor. As the subject failed to give correct answers to the instructor's questions, the volunteer was told to give higher and higher electric shocks. As the shocks increased, the actor pretending to be the subject would bang on the wall in feigned agony, complain about his heart condition and, eventually, as the shocks increased to the normally fatal level of 450 volts, fall silent. If the volunteer hesitated in administering the electric shocks, a white-coated "instructor" (in reality, another actor) told the volunteer that they must continue. If at any time the unwitting volunteer asked to halt the experiment, he was told, successively, by the "instructor":

1. Please continue.
2. The experiment requires that you continue.
3. It is absolutely essential that you continue.
4. You have no other choice, you must go on.

If the volunteer still wished to stop after all four successive verbal injunctions, the experiment was halted. Otherwise, it was halted after the volunteer had given the maximum 450-volt shock three times in succession. Of Milgram's subjects, 65 percent (twenty-six out of forty) administered the experiment's final—and theoretically fatal—450-volt shock. Only one participant refused to administer shocks *before* the 300-volt level. Notably, all were told during the experiment that they would not be held responsible for what happened.

Traditionally, and by Milgram himself, this experiment has been cited to demonstrate the pernicious effects of authority upon moral conduct. If people are told to do something awful by someone who is clearly in authority—in this case, a professorial type in a white coat—all too often they do it. But another lesson is also evident in the fact that the volunteers who administered the electric shocks, crucially, were told that they had no responsibility for the results.

The nasty human truth of Milgram's experiment has been demonstrated many times in recent history. Mass warfare offers many examples. During World War II, German reservists were called up by the government to join regular military units but also police units, like Reserve Police Battalion 101. The members of this unit were "ordinary men": teachers, bankers and plumbers drawn from a wide variety of backgrounds, from across Germany. As is the way with groups put into difficult circumstances together, the battalion quickly bonded into a close-knit team. The battalion was deployed to the Eastern Front, where it followed closely behind the Wehrmacht advance across Eastern Europe and into the Soviet Union.

The battalion was not recruited on any particular ideological basis, though some were also members of the Nazi party (a good percentage of Germans were at the time). But these were not Waffen-SS ideologues; they were largely middle-aged men with wives and families, gardens and pet dogs.

The battalion, in other words, was unexceptional, banal (as Hannah Arendt might have put it).[1] In a little over a year, this battalion of approximately five hundred "ordinary men" killed thirty-eight thousand Jews and dispatched approximately forty-five thousand more to extermination camps.[2] The battalion did most of its killing by shooting civilians at close range after rounding them up from villages and towns overrun by German forces. In the course of this murderous spree, not one member of the battalion questioned the orders or sought to leave the unit. When given the option by commanders to opt out of specific opportunities for mass murder, fewer than fifteen men of five hundred did so.

The Milgram experiment was recently repeated, to test how people today might submit to authority when ordered to inflict pain upon innocent others.[3] As reported in the journal *American Psychologist*, Professor Jerry Burger replicated part of the Milgram study—but stopping at 150 volts, the moment at which the subject cries out to stop—to see whether people today would still obey.[4] There were some changes to account for modern ethical rules and social sensibilities. University ethics committees barred researchers from pushing the unwitting subjects through to an imaginary lethal 450 volts as Milgram had done.

But despite these restrictions, the results were very much the same. As in the 1960s, more than half the participants agreed to proceed with the experiment past the 150-volt mark. Burger interviewed the participants afterward and found that those who stopped generally believed themselves to be responsible for the shocks, whereas those who kept going tended to hold the experimenter accountable. This reveals a crucial distinction: It was the participants' assumption for relinquishing of agency that determined their actions.

Milgram's experiment is today so well known that it has entered the collective consciousness—but for the wrong reason. Although the experiment is generally viewed as demonstrating the pernicious effects of authority, in fact it reveals a more important truth: that when people feel no agency and no responsibility for their actions, they can commit horrific crimes. The Milgram experiment nevertheless seems remote from our normal lives. One problem with such an experiment is that it is hard to imagine ourselves in a situation where we would have to give electric shocks to an innocent person. But the uncomfortable truth is that such situations do not come announced; the chance to perform cruelty upon others comes disguised. I know this now because I was once in a position of one of Milgram's test subjects, asked to inflict suffering upon others. Except in my case, unlike his experiment, the suffering was real.

For almost as long as I remember, I have wanted to be a diplomat. As a schoolboy, I read *The Times* (of London) every day, pretty much all the way through, gripped by its accounts of détente, the proxy wars between East and West and the terrifying, yet intriguing, calculus of nuclear war: first strikes, the "missile gap" and the strange but compelling logic of Mutually Assured Destruction. Thanks to inherited color blindness, I couldn't fulfill my original ambition to become a fighter pilot. The next-best thing would be to become a diplomat and enter this weighty but arcane and closed world, to learn its terminologies and codes.

I was, moreover, fired by emotional urges. My family exuded a certain awe of "the Foreign Office" where British diplomats worked: Several relations had tried and failed to enter the elite ranks of the diplomatic corps. One childhood memory stands out. At perhaps age twelve, I announced to my family that I wanted to become a diplomat. My father, who later denied having said this, turned to me and said, "You have to be very clever to become a diplomat." Thus was my ambition sealed.

University came and went. Eventually, I managed to enter the fast stream of the Foreign Office, a tiny group: some twenty-odd of the many thousands who applied. We were a chosen elite, given to expect that in due course we would become ambassadors and undersecretaries, the most senior exponents of our country's wishes. I was elated to join this exclusive club and happy to undergo the many compromises membership in this group entailed.

Among them was the process that all new entrants must undertake in order to join the foreign service, and therein become party to the state's secrets. "Positive vetting" is a deeply intrusive examination of friendships, family relations, habits and personal history designed to discover whether the proposed new diplomat poses any kind of security risk.

To check its prospective sharers of secrets, the Security Department of the Foreign Office assigned an investigator to examine my personal background, quiz acquaintances and friends, in order to find out whether my behavior, past or present, might render me vulnerable to approaches from foreign intelligence services. Without this clearance, the would-be diplomat cannot begin work since a great deal of work in the "office," as it soon became known to me, involves access to Top Secret material, the compromise of which, in theory at least, poses a grave risk to the security of the state.

Others who had gone before told me that the process was straightforward "as long as you don't tell them anything." Unfortunately for me, my personal referees had already told my investigator various things, including the fact that I occasionally drank too much at university, played poker and that I was sharing a flat with a gay man. I took the naive view that since I had nothing in my life to be ashamed of, I would tell them the truth. This approach proved to be a serious mistake.

My vetting took place almost exactly as the Cold War was ending, in 1989. But the Foreign Office still feared the corrupting attentions of the KGB and others, and it was felt that being homosexual, which I am not, risked exposing the officer to blackmail. It did not seem to have occurred to the mandarins in charge of Security Department that a blanket prohibition on homosexuality was more likely to force acting or potential foreign service officers to lie about their true sexual natures and thus increase their vulnerability to blackmail. So my vetting officer subjected me to a long series of absurd and insulting questions about my sexuality, culminating in the conclusive, "So you've never been tempted off the straight and narrow, then?"

Meanwhile, my investigator had found out from application forms that my grandmother was Polish. Poland was at that time undergoing its transformation to democracy. But the Security Department suspected, following policy, that the mere fact that I had Polish relations posed a security risk, since the KGB might "get at" them and use them to "get at" me (it had happened in the past when Poland was a vassal of the Soviet Union). My family was thus forced to dig up long-buried records and tell the awful investigator exactly when, where and how all my Polish ancestors had died, in order that the KGB couldn't discover their names and impersonate them to "get at" me. This led to the upsetting discovery that some of my Polish forebears, captured as members of the Polish resistance, had died in Auschwitz.

I was obliged to attend several interviews with the investigator in a sparse office in an anonymous building near Parliament Square, furnished with sinister-looking steel filing cabinets. His desk, like that of an interrogator, was bare but for one government-issue swivel lamp, the only light in the otherwise gloomy room. Sometimes the interviews would last for hours. My family and friends, who were subjected to separate questionings, were at first amused by his questions, but soon became irritated and in some cases upset.

The planned start date of my work at the Foreign Office came and went and I had not passed my "PV," as positive vetting is known. The personnel officer assigned to my case took some pleasure in telling me that it was extremely unlikely that I would eventually be allowed in. I considered withdrawing from the process and abandoning my application to join, but I decided instead to swallow these humiliations. Too badly I wanted to become that rarefied species, a diplomat.

In retrospect, this process was akin to a kind of "hazing" ritual, of the kind practiced in certain American colleges, the military or similar institutions. It was a form of ritual humiliation, where my sexual habits, personal finances and most intimate relations were probed and exposed. Once complete, not only was I permitted to join the elite club of those permitted to see state secrets; I felt that I had shared with them—through my investigator—something of me, something private and personal. This was more, much more than a regular induction into a job.

The inculcation went further when the new entrant to the diplomatic service entered training. Immediately, we were encouraged to undergo a subtle but crucial transformation: the "I" became "we." In describing to us the arcane and fetishized practices of the foreign service (the use, for instance, of special paper for ministers and senior officials: green-colored paper called, perversely, "blue"), our instructors did not talk of how they saw things with the personal and individual "I." Instead, they talked about how "we" saw the world. Telegrams, then the principal form of communication between the Foreign Office and British embassies worldwide (there are now "e-grams"), were written in the first person plural. The author did not describe his or her own view of politics in Iran; instead they described how "we" saw the prospects for engagement with the Islamic regime.

A young diplomat from the British High Commission* in Preto-

---

*In former colonies that are now members of the British Commonwealth, British representations are known not as embassies but as High Commissions.

ria lectured the new entrants about how "we" thought sanctions on apartheid South Africa were a bad idea (these were the days of Margaret Thatcher's policy of "constructive engagement" with the white minority regime). A diplomatic dispatch was presented to us as an example of how to write such pieces. In it, the ambassador wrote about how "we" had got Iran "wrong" and "we" needed a new approach. In a number of different ways, the new recruits were taught how "we" saw the world. What we were never taught, however, was *why* it was that "we" saw the world that way. This method was assumed, implied, never confessed but nonetheless supreme.

One training exercise involved a game revolving around a crisis in a fictional country, Boremeya, and what "we," meaning Britain, should do about it. It was a good game, and fun. It lasted about a day and consisted of crisis meetings, submissions to ministers ("Make sure to use 'blue' paper!") and difficult encounters with the Boremeyan foreign minister, played by one of our instructors. Throughout the game, the new entrants were told to consider what "we" wanted or needed in the situation. Within such exercises, and infused in all our training, was a clear, if only rarely explicit, assumption. As diplomats, "we" were the embodiment of the state, Britain. What we thought was right was thus implicitly right for Britain.

It is obvious to the reader that such a transformation from the individual to the group must imply a loss both of individual agency and of moral autonomy. Processes such as that I underwent to join the Foreign Office have parallels in military induction, including in more striking form, Reserve Police Battalion 101. But it was not obvious to me at the time. I still felt the same person. I still believed that I was autonomous and free to make my own choices, within certain limits that I freely accepted. I convinced myself that if faced with a morally unacceptable instruction, such as murdering Jews, I would have the courage to refuse. Little did I know that today's moral choices rarely come so clearly signaled.

I HAD BEEN IN THE FOREIGN SERVICE some nine years by the time I was posted to the British Mission to the United Nations in New York. By then I was deeply steeped in the culture and mind-habits of my institution. Many of my friends were in the Foreign Office. The "office," as we called it, was a kind of brother-and-sisterhood: All over the world there were co-members with whom I shared a common language and experience. I had experienced with them excitement and boredom, from the corridors of the United Nations to the mountains of the Hindu Kush. I was with them as they wept the frustrations of negotiations, and as gunfire crackled on the streets of Pristina. They have been at my side in Hebron and Dresden, Oslo and Islamabad. With them, I watched wars begin and end, wrote and argued international law, and shared the many joys and miseries of a life lived in the glamour of overseas embassies, of high-level meetings and the dinginess of Whitehall offices. It was not an ordinary job.

And my job in New York was not ordinary either. I was to be the head of the Middle East section at the British Mission to the UN. It was an exciting and challenging task. My responsibilities covered the Arab–Israel dispute, the 1988 Lockerbie bombing by Libyan agents, and the long-standing and unresolved injustice of Morocco's occupation of the Western Sahara. But my primary responsibility was Iraq—ensuring its disarmament and containment after the 1990 war, and the sanctions agreed at the UN Security Council to effect these goals. For Britain at the UN in those days, there was no more important task, and it was my responsibility. In the early days of my posting, I was so excited by the prospect of my work that I would whoop with joy as water poured over me in my morning shower.

One central part of my job was to maintain the UN Security Council's support of restrictive economic sanctions against Iraq. When first told of this task, I relished it. I had no question that the sanctions were justified. Their purpose was, after all, to punish and contain that most evil and lawless of dictators, Saddam Hussein. When briefed in London before my posting, however, the first doubts began to assert themselves. Sanctions on Iraq had been imposed, I naively thought, because Iraq had not disarmed itself of its infamous "weapons of mass destruction" (WMD), in this case defined as nuclear, chemical and biological weapons, and ballistic missiles with a range of over 150 kilometers. This failure presented a clear case for the maintenance of sanctions. However, when I asked one of my briefing officers in London whether the UK believed Iraq maintained significant stocks of WMD, he looked a little sheepish. "Not really," he replied. How, then, do we justify sanctions, I asked, trying to contain my astonishment. He replied, on the basis that Iraq had failed to answer multiple questions about the destruction of its earlier stocks. In summary, sanctions were in place because Iraq had not correctly answered questions.

By the end of 1997, when I joined the mission, British and American policy at the UN Security Council was under severe pressure. Iraq's allies on the council, particularly France and Russia, were arguing for an easing of sanctions on the grounds that Iraq had complied fully with its obligations, following the Gulf War cease-fire, to disarm completely of its nuclear program, chemical and biological weapons and long-range missiles. The UN weapons inspectors were, however, clearly saying that this was not the case, and that there remained many unresolved issues about Iraq's WMD. We, the U.S. and the UK, deployed these unresolved issues to argue support for sanctions— what had happened to all the missiles Iraq had imported? Why the discrepancy between chemical bombs produced and those verifiably destroyed? Et cetera, et cetera. Sanctions, we argued with great vigor, were necessary to force Iraq to disarm, fully and verifiably, as it had demonstrably not yet done. It was a tough diplomatic fight, not helped by the absence of hard evidence.

Though opponents of sanctions argued that they were unjustified and caused immense human suffering in Iraq, our counterarguments were plausible: Iraq had failed on numerous occasions to cooperate fully with the weapons inspectors, leaving important questions un- answered; Saddam Hussein obstructed the operation of the UN's oil-for-food program, which was designed to lessen the humanitarian suffering.

It was my job to cull and collate the innumerable statistics, reports and testimonies in support of this latter version of the story and to deploy them in speeches and debates in the Security Council. On the other side of the table, the diplomats opposing sanctions—led by Russia and France—could cite myriad reports detailing the suffering under the sanctions regime and the inequities of the oil-for-food program.

It was, of course, a complex story that we managed to divide into two distinct and opposing narratives. The atmosphere between the delegations on the Security Council was aggressive and adversarial, as it remained until—and after—the 2003 invasion. Political divi- sions were allowed to degenerate into personal animosities. The coun- cil, its chambers and corridors became a diplomatic battle zone where the more we fought, the more we entrenched our positions into com- peting blacks and whites. Thus were we able to obscure the deeper truth.

Governments and their officials can compose convincing versions of the truth, filled with more or less verifiable facts, and yet be entirely wrong. I did not make up lies about Hussein's smuggling or obstruction of the UN's humanitarian program. The speeches I drafted for my ambassador to deliver to the Security Council and my telegrams back to London were composed of facts filtered from the stacks of reports and intelligence that daily hit my desk. As I read these reports, facts and judgments that contradicted "our" version of events would fade into nothingness. Facts that reinforced our narrative would stand out to me as if highlighted, to be later deployed by me, my ambassador and my ministers, like hand grenades in the diplomatic trench warfare. Details in otherwise complicated reports would be extracted to be telegraphed back to London, where they would be inserted into ministerial briefings or press articles. A complicated picture was reduced to a selection of facts that became factoids, such as the suggestion that Saddam Hussein imported huge quantities of whiskey or built a dozen palaces, validated by constant repetition: true, but not the whole truth.

In the end, it became clear even to us that comprehensive sanctions were counterproductive. They targeted the wrong group of people, and their effects undermined the necessary international support for the containment of the Saddam regime. This reality slowly percolated into our small policy-making group, and eventually led to a change in policy. As the century turned, the U.S. and the UK initiated a shift in Security Council policy toward what became known as "smart sanctions"—whereby Iraq could import all civilian goods except those with potential military application: so-called dual-use goods. But by then, the damage had been done.

That damage has been more fully revealed since the 2003 U.S.-led invasion of Iraq. One assumption of those planning that war was that

Iraq's middle class would quickly recover from Saddam's removal, and the economy would rapidly thrive. That assumption quickly met the brute force of the reality that there was no longer an Iraqi middle class, and no economy to speak of. Iraq's non-oil economy had been more or less completely destroyed by the dozen years of sanctions that I, and others, had helped enforce. Anyone with the chance— mostly the educated and professional classes—had left. Within a year of the imposition of sanctions, Iraq's GDP had dropped by about three-quarters of its 1990 value to approximately that of the 1940s. By 1996, one million children under five were malnourished. In a country that had been cholera free, by 1994 there were 1,344 cases per 100,000 people. Even after the oil-for-food program came into operation, water treatment plants lacked the proper spare parts and maintenance; there were extended power cuts. The population had no choice but to obtain water directly from contaminated rivers, re-sulting in turn in massive increases in water-borne diseases such as typhoid and cholera. Though the statistics are debated still, and data from Iraq during this period are unreliable, a recent and thorough academic history of the sanctions era concludes from a review of epidemiological studies that for the period from 1990 to 2003, there was an "excess mortality rate" of more than 500,000 for children under five. In other words, half a million children died.[5] Though Saddam Hussein doubtless had a hand too, I cannot avoid my own responsibility. This was my work; this is what I did.

I HAVE NO WAY TO ASSUAGE the shame I feel when I contemplate this episode. I was aware of the reports of humanitarian suffering, but I did little about them. In discussion within my ministry, I may have occasionally argued for easing the effects of comprehensive sanctions.

But if I did, I suspect that I argued the political grounds for such a shift—the loss of support for our policies—rather than the urgent moral and humanitarian arguments. In our ministry's culture, it was often deemed "emotional" or "immature" to burden arguments with moral sentiment. Real diplomats were cold-eyed and hardheaded, immune to the arguments of liberal protesters, journalists and other softheads who did not understand how the "real world" worked.

For years afterward, I wondered how this might have happened. Why did we permit this? Or rather, the actual, direct but more uncomfortable question: Why did I do this? My colleagues and I were decent people, or so I preferred to think. Likewise, my ministers and officials who endorsed the policy and defended it in Parliament and before an increasingly critical press. It was this very decency that helped still my doubts, that persuaded me that we could not have been doing wrong. Later, in recounting this story, my former colleagues or friends would say, "You were doing what you were told," implying thereby that I bore no guilt and, needless to say, that they bore none either.

And as in all institutions unscrutinized from outside, the hold of "groupthink" was a firm one upon our little group of policy makers—no more than half a dozen or so people in the British government, a few more in the U.S. We reassured one another that we were doing the right thing. Our arguments sounded all the better the more we rehearsed them to one another.

The comfortable succor of my institution, in this case the British Foreign Office, allowed me to ignore the dictates of my own conscience. My bosses and colleagues were to me as the white-coated instructor in the Milgram experiment. The man who knew better. The man who held authority. Paid and committed to my profession and its enveloping persona, I was more than happy to press the button.

But here the parallel with Milgram ends. Milgram was an experiment. No one was hurt. Nothing really happened except a point was proven. Sanctions on Iraq were, unfortunately, no experiment. Though the arguments we played out in stuffy rooms in the UN in New York often seemed abstract, the effects of sanctions on ordinary men, women and children were to them all too painful. In the end, the difference between what I did and the Milgram experiment was this: In Milgram's case, the victim being "electrocuted" was an actor. In my case, the screams of pain and anguish coming from the other side of the wall were real.

The "man in the white coat" problem, as the insight from Milgram's experiment might be called, is not just a problem of diplomacy. It takes little imagination to see how, to varying degrees, it is a problem intrinsic to any system where people feel dissociated from the consequences of their actions—where they feel that someone else, not them, is really in control. Thus, the ultimate paradox of government, however well-meaning in intent, is revealed. The more government seeks to act to tackle particular problems, the less individuals are likely to feel responsible for them. Whatever is legal is thus rendered morally permissible. Evidence for this is all around us in the decaying standards of public behavior in many realms, from the shameless greed of Wall Street bankers, to the brutality and exploitation perpetuated in the anonymity of the World Wide Web, to the thuggish antics to be witnessed on public transportation.

The answer is obvious. Confront individuals with the consequences of their actions. Restore the moral understanding that each of us is responsible for the world as it is, and for each other. Take away the man in the white coat.

6

WHY CHESS IS AN INAPPROPRIATE METAPHOR FOR INTERNATIONAL RELATIONS, WHY JACKSON POLLOCK PAINTINGS ARE A BETTER BUT STILL INADEQUATE METAPHOR, AND WHY THIS HAS PROFOUND POLITICAL CONSEQUENCES

The chess game is a frequent metaphor for the business of international relations. Artfully shot photographs of kings and knights adorn many a book or scholarly article (particularly those about the theory of "IR"). The chess game appeals as analogy because it is complicated and involves two clearly defined opponents and, above all, because although a very difficult game, it is ultimately comprehensible: There may be a very large number of permutations (according to Garry Kasparov, there are 10^{120} possible games), but there are a limited number of outcomes. Computers can be programmed to play chess as well as if not better than the best human players.

Such metaphors, therefore, have a reassuring quality: If the game is played well by a state, a government, they will win, or at least prevent a loss—as long as our players, or computers and software, are good enough. The shape and possibilities of the pieces and board are known and finite. It's comforting to think that foreign policy is a bit like pulling a lever, and after some whirring and clicking, a result pops out at the other end. Historians and commentators reinforce this suggestion. Their articles and books abound with the linear narrative: Decision A leads to policy B leads to outcome C; if Washington adopts policy *x*, result *y* will surely follow.

Maps and atlases evoke a similar effect. None of them portrays a world as it is: No globe is big enough. Jorge Luis Borges suggested such a map in his wonderful story "Of Exactitude in Science": a map to the scale of the Earth, with every manhole cover, every goat path, depicted as it actually *is*. Such a map would be perfectly accurate but of course wholly useless. All depictions must therefore reduce and thereby distort. All maps are nonetheless imbued with a certain implied confidence that their delineations are meaningful and significant. The neatly drawn lines, dots and shadings convey a message that the world is ultimately known and demarcated, complicated but clearly defined.

There are several problems with the chess metaphor, and indeed with the conventional way of thinking about international relations. In the discomforting reality of the world today, the number of relevant actors who may affect the outcome is invariably far greater than two, the potential moves of these multiple players is unlimited, and therefore the number of possible interactions in a globalized world is certainly greater than 10^{120}, even though this is already an unimaginably big number.

Multiply the billions of connected humans in today's world by the actions available to them, then throw in the reactions and counterreactions to these initial actions, run the calculation for even a short while, and you will end up with an impossibly large number of possible outcomes. That number is massive and possibly infinite; there are probably insufficient atoms in the universe to equal it. Given this reality, the hope of a foreign policy of deliberate action to produce predictable results looks increasingly vain. Instead of pulling a lever on a machine to produce a predictable result, making foreign policy starts to look more like a roll of the dice—or more accurately, selecting a number between one and infinity.

Few dare acknowledge what increasingly appears to be the truth that the world has no defined shape, aside from its continents, rivers and oceans, and even these shift form and location, now at an alarming speed. That instead of a chessboard or a web, it is in fact a swirling miasma of billions upon billions of interactions, not on a fixed pattern, or a net, but an ever-changing mesh of connections, some significant but temporary, some long-lasting but inconsequential, a reality more evocative of the swirls and spatters of a Jackson Pollock painting than a chessboard.

When we look at some illustrations drawn from this maelstrom, you'll see the dilemma. . . .

In 2009, a spate of high-profile kidnappings in Phoenix left Arizona the kidnapping capital of the United States. That same year, eighteen people were killed in Mexico City after a gang of hooded gunmen attacked a local drug treatment facility, apparently a refuge for rival gang members. The connection between these two phenomena was a seemingly harmless U.S. policy aimed at improving border enforcement with Mexico. The policy was designed in part to placate a domestic constituency alarmed at high rates of illegal immigration. But it had the adverse and unexpected consequence of aggravating a series of drug wars in Mexico. By slowing migration from Mexico, so too it slowed the transfer of drugs to the north. But as drug supply in the U.S. fell, supplies increased dramatically in Mexico, lowering domestic prices and fueling a spike in local drug consumption. Over the next months, gang-related violence and kidnappings surged as new and old gangs alike sought to mark out their turf in the newly developing marketplace. With thousands dead and the violence spreading back to American territory, U.S. policy makers are now forced to contend with the unintended consequences of actions once thought to bring greater stability to America's southern border.

It is now well known that Osama bin Laden's involvement in the battle of the Afghan mujahideen against the Soviet army served as the springboard for Al Qaeda's campaign of global jihad. The defeat of that army's occupation of Afghanistan, among other factors, helped contribute to the fall of the Berlin Wall and the collapse of the Soviet empire. Though bin Laden and Saddam Hussein were wholly unconnected, the 9/11 attacks created the political momentum for the invasion of Iraq.* That invasion indirectly led to the de facto separation of Iraq's Kurdish north, the rise of Iran as the dominant regional power and, likely and tragically, the demise of the Christian community in Iraq, driven out by sectarian violence. None of these outcomes was predicted, even by the invasion's most imaginative planners.

The weapons and influence of Al Qaeda were a function of bin Laden's personal wealth, which was itself a consequence of his father's large fortune, made from building for the royal family and others well connected in oil-rich Saudi Arabia, his home country, a long-

---

*As the UK's Middle East and Iraq "expert" at the UN from 1998 to 2002, I was required to read a thick folder of intelligence every day on Iraq, its WMD and efforts to rearm. There was not a single report suggesting a connection between the Saddam regime and Al Qaeda, nor would such a connection be plausible given the radically different natures of these entities—one secular and Ba'athist, the other fundamentalist and Islamist. The head of Britain's Secret Intelligence Service (often known as MI6) also confirmed the absence of connection.

standing U.S. ally. The "original" Al Qaeda, as some analysts now call it, has meanwhile spawned several deadly affiliates or "franchises," a name reminiscent of the spread of McDonald's burger restaurants— Al Qaeda in the Islamic Maghreb (AQIM), Al Qaeda in the Arabian Peninsula (AQAP), AQ in Somalia, AQ in Afghanistan, the "Nigerian Taliban" Boko Haram, and terrorist groups without names in London and Miami—and has helped inspire murderous attacks from Fort Hood, Texas, to Bali and Mumbai. One of the planners of the Mumbai rampage, which cost nearly two hundred lives, was an American who also, it turns out, was for a while an agent for America's Drug Enforcement Agency, which wanted his help in locating heroin suppliers in Pakistan. The DEA, it appears, failed to inform other parts of the massive U.S. intelligence machinery.

Elsewhere, Al Qaeda is also loosely associated with, and serves as inspiration for, the Al Shabaab Islamist militia, which currently controls much of southern and central Somalia.

Here, the insatiable global appetite for fish has driven international fishing fleets—from Japan, Russia and Europe—to plunder Somalia's unprotected waters, denying a livelihood to Somalia's many coastal fishermen. Partly as a result (there are other reasons too), some have turned to piracy, hijacking vessels in a lucrative trade that a substantial flotilla of heavily armed ultramodern warships deployed in the area has failed so far to prevent. This naval fleet, sometimes numbering as many as twenty or more vessels, embodies unprecedented international cooperation, including warships from former antagonists such as Russia, NATO, India and China. "Combined Task Force 150" also includes the European Union's first-ever joint naval deployment. But so far, this unique and expensive military collaboration has failed to stop or deter the pirates. More people were taken hostage at sea in 2010 than in any previous year on record.[1]

Some of the proceeds of that piracy, where ship owners often pay several million dollars to liberate their captured vessels and crews, have found their way to Al Shabaab, which has used the money to purchase weapons with which to fight its insurgency against the internationally backed Somali Transitional Federal Government in Mogadishu. Young men are now traveling from the U.S., Britain and elsewhere to train with Al Shabaab and its piracy-funded weapons. National security agencies—MI5, the FBI—have warned of the danger that these radicalized young men pose on their return to their "home" countries, trained and ready to commit further acts of violence. In late 2010, a young Somali-American sought to detonate a bomb at a Christmas tree lighting ceremony in Portland, Oregon.

Such effects are inherently unpredictable and can appear random, even though some causes and some effects are, at least in retrospect, discernible. They do not follow the neat patterns of a flow chart or a mathematical equation. Though multiple and complex, the model of a chess game is no more appropriate, either. What we witness in the world is not ordered, at least in a sequential, logical fashion, but neither is it chaos. It is entirely wrong to say that the pattern of cause and effect in the world today is chaotic or anarchic, even if sometimes it seems that way. It may *resemble* chaos, but in fact it is a hugely complex and dynamic mesh of multiple cause and effect and back again (even Jackson Pollock paintings have an underlying order). Given this reality, any model or any metaphor may oversimplify and thus distort this nature—an artificial simplicity imposed upon complexity.

Only later will historians, masters of the reductive art of the narrative, be able to put shape to what seems today formless, and even then they will be capturing but a tiny part of what constitutes existence now. For now, a better depiction suggests itself, a fantastic mélange with ends and connections that shift, merge and disappear. To shape this mesh, to put form to it, to give it names, is to change it, to reduce it and ultimately to fail to understand it completely. Unfortunately, this is precisely what governments are required to do.

IT IS CONVENTIONAL WISDOM that with myriad international problems that cross frontiers, the world needs ever more international diplomacy and engagement. But it may be, in fact, that we need less, at least of the kind that currently predominates—the lattice of state-to-state relations and multilateral institutions.

There are now a great many international negotiation processes addressing a bewildering array of problems, from the familiar— climate change, nuclear proliferation—to the obscure—postal standards and the standardization of measurements. But on the most acute and urgent problems, the evidence is mounting that these processes are not delivering the necessary results—effective solutions to the world's international problems. The measure of the effectiveness of this form of politics must be as for any form of politics: What are the outputs? What are the real effects on real problems and people?

The climate change "process," with its summits at Copenhagen (2009) and Cancún (2010), has involved hundreds of meetings and thousands of delegates and, on more than one occasion, "world leaders." But the process has yet to produce any substantive agreement, let alone concrete and plausibly effective measures, to reduce atmospheric carbon, despite the vast expenditure of negotiating energy and voluminous reams of treaty text and media commentary. Meanwhile, the concentration of carbon in the atmosphere continues to rise.

The G8 Gleneagles Summit in 2005 was notable for the extraordinary length and height of fences erected, and the ten thousand police required, to keep protesters away from the tiny group of decision makers meeting in the remote Scottish location. The summiteers themselves sought to make history by their commitment to $50 billion in new aid money. This announcement was claimed to "make poverty history," echoing the rhetoric of the huge "Make Poverty History" campaign, which culminated in several massive "Live 8" concerts that summer, where those enjoying the music in person or on television were encouraged to lobby their leaders by sending them text messages asking them to relieve Third World debt. At the UN World Summit later that year, all member states of the UN recommitted themselves to the goal of reducing absolute poverty by half by 2015—the headline target of the so-called Millennium Development Goals (MDG).

It is depressing to relate the utter failure of those making these commitments to keep to them.[2] Of those making the Gleneagles declaration, all serious countries and seven of them more or less democracies, not one fulfilled the promise they had made. Five years after Gleneagles, it was estimated that G8 pledges would fall short by $20 billion.[3] The U.S. and European Union had done virtually nothing to remove the import barriers and agricultural subsidies that do much to stymie economic growth in developing countries. By 2010, the G8 itself, perhaps out of embarrassment, had ceased mentioning its aid goals in its communiqués. It did, however, make play of yet another new "initiative," this time to target maternal health. The most recent assessment of the MDG is that they will certainly not be attained, an unsurprising assessment given the paltry efforts made by the signatories of the UN declaration to substantiate their rhetoric. Of one thing, however, we can be sure: There will be more such declarations, freshened up with new slogans and impassioned speeches, or tweets, or Facebook pages, or whatever, in future.

The recent financial crisis has occasioned massed bouts of international hand-wringing over global regulation of banking and investment. The G20 gatherings have emerged as the leading forum to discuss such measures, clearly necessary to manage the out-of-control flows of unintelligible financial instruments, like the infamous "collateralized debt obligations" (CDOs) that spread risk with no oversight. But despite repeated meetings, communiqués and speeches, here too no effective policy response has emerged. It has instead become clear that the financial industry's lobbyists in each country have conspired to ensure that every government is unwilling to trade its supposed competitive advantage for collective measures, like globally agreed and sufficient capital requirements for lenders. To satisfy public concern, instead these meetings offer "commitments" to effective controls, and "processes" to discuss them—no doubt without cease until the next crisis erupts. Thus, the impression of activity is created, the absence of concrete action obscured.

Given the gravity of the problems that these international processes are supposed to address, and yet their feeble outputs, it's urgent to consider what's going on. The cynical might argue that these processes are simply rackets run by the powerful, who have no intrinsic interest in success. In its own way, this is a comforting and self-serving excuse that requires little response save cynicism on our part. But my own experience of diplomacy and international negotiation suggests something more subtle is the problem.

Invariably, when these negotiations and conferences fail, commentators are quick to point fingers at one participant or other for derailing the process: the Chinese for eviscerating the Copenhagen climate change talks, France for blocking Security Council authority for the invasion of Iraq in 2003. But these accusations may be missing the point: The problem of international diplomacy is not the actors within it, though their actions may hint at the more sub-merged problem. The real problem may be concealed within the very system itself. Indeed, the problem may *be* the system.

Diplomacy is a system. Any system—like a club—requires certain characteristics in order to participate. And it reinforces these characteristics merely by existing and by requiring its members to exhibit these characteristics. The current international system comprises the conventional institutions of diplomacy. From these institutions, we can see clearly what characteristics are required to participate.

Diplomacy and international relations are, by their nature, about *nation states.* The United Nations, the European Union, ASEAN, the World Trade Organization, the G20 are all associations of states. This may seem a very obvious and trite point to emphasize, but it is essential. For my experience suggests that states, and their exponents, do not accurately reflect what humans are about, nor what they want. Thus, it is naive to expect that their machinations, in the form of interstate diplomacy, will produce results consistent with humanity's needs in general.

This problem takes several different forms, and the evidence for it, if you choose to look, is manifold. The first is that the connection between what states do and say in international negotiations and what their populations think is now extremely tenuous, to say the least. In democracies, the international representative of the state is accountable to their home ministry, which is led by a politician who is accountable to the legislature, which is ultimately accountable to the population which elects its members. This is already a very long chain of explanation and accountability.

A good example of an acutely important but complicated issue is Iraq policy. My experience dealing with Iraq policy was that only the very small group on the front lines of the policy had any hope of a comprehensive grasp of the many and diverse issues at stake: WMD, sanctions, international law, the dynamics of the UN Security Council, to mention just a few, all of which themselves were extraordinarily complicated. My ministers, whose job it was to explain and "sell" the policy in public and to Parliament, usually had only a very general and hazy grasp of the subject. In Parliament, there were no MPs who could equal the officials' knowledge and expertise, and thus properly hold them to account. In any case, during the four and a half years that I worked on Iraq policy inside the British government, I was never questioned by any MP directly about my work, nor did any journalist ever closely question me with any serious expertise. The picture in the U.S. is similar.

One consequence of this extraordinarily dissociated chain between diplomat and citizen is that the diplomat can have no accurate idea of what the citizen wants. Hence, this requires diplomats to assume, or rather, *invent* what they think the citizen—his nation— wants. I know this because I did this myself many times. It is a function of the inculcation process diplomats must go through to join and then embody their profession—the assumption that "we" know best. Diplomats, by the nature of their job, are encouraged to believe that they can determine what is in their nation's interests, without consulting those in whose name they claim to be operating.

This process of assuming or inventing the desires and requirements of a state, often called "interests," is usually conducted in secret by exchange of telegrams or classified e-mails, or in policy submissions to senior officials and political masters. I have participated many times in such exercises. With exquisite concision, the official will describe the issue at hand, then he or she will articulate what is at stake for "us"—our "interests," in short. In recent years, it has become fashionable for the exponents of foreign policy to talk about "values" as important in diplomacy—things like democracy and human rights. But in truth, the underlying calculus remains little changed, as does the diplomatic mind-set, and this is no surprise, for it is only natural for the exponent of the state to think in terms of what his state needs and wants; it is to the diplomat as to a cow eating grass or mooing; it is what they *do*.

It would be absurd for a diplomat to adopt a different set of criteria to guide their work and policies, and would certainly guarantee a short career. Such interests typically, and by inherited tradition, take the form of a hierarchy of priorities where security—the requirement to secure the state and its population—ranks at the top, followed by economic interests. There is little rigor in these delineations and orderings, and indeed only rarely do officials distinguish between types of interest, instead talking in more general terms about what "we" may want in any given situation. The identification between diplomat and state cannot be overemphasized. While both security and economic interests would fit onto most people's lists of what is important, only a very few people would, I suspect, declare them as paramount in all situations or as their sole requirements in any situation.

The premise of the international system, and of the state exponents who populate it, is a fundamentally incredible one—that the needs and wants of the Earth's billions of people can be boiled down into separate and discrete subsets of interests which can then be meaningfully arbitrated. This is difficult to grasp because we have become so acclimatized to the state-based system: the international diplomatic forums with their neatly lettered name cards adorning serried rows at the UN General Assembly or European Council. But reflect for a moment and the absurdity becomes clear: How can a tiny group of people possibly know what is best for their country of millions? By extension, it is equally implausible to expect that a collection of such tiny groups, meeting at, say, the UN or the G20, can produce meaningful and effective agreements for the whole globe. The disconnection is simply too great. They are required to assume, to guess. They know it, as I knew it. But it is the rest who believe it.

The problem is more insidious and damaging in its effects than merely this. The requirement of the system is that the needs and wants of the world's peoples are reduced into such subsets—a reductive requirement. That need to reduce the complexity of reality into simplicity imposes upon the diplomats and other denizens of the system an unnatural and distorting burden—to turn their understanding of the world, and our needs upon it, into something else: the calculus of states. Most of the time this process is invisible, assumed and unremarked upon. Only occasionally are its aberrations so gross that they break the surface of our indifference—for me, it was the experience of Iraq sanctions where I realized, and only in retrospect, the gross divide between my own beliefs and understanding of what was right, and the way I was required to think—and do—at the time.

There is an additional negative consequence of this state-dominated mode of thinking. The chess game requires two sides to be played: white and black. The process of simplifying and overstating our own needs, known as calculating our interests, requires a reciprocal technique. If there is to be an "Us," there must also be a "Them."

This happened on the Iraq sanctions issue at the UN Security Council, where the diplomats gaily perpetuated the national divisions between opposing delegations, even when there were no facts to disagree over. I was a willing participant in this farce: The UK/U.S. would veto proposals made by the "other" side, in this case France and Russia, even if we ourselves had made the very same proposal a few weeks earlier and they had blocked them. The effect of such essentializing, the segregation of ourselves into two competing sides, was not to reduce conflict, but to perpetuate it.

It is no coincidence that it is governments that perform this essentializing. They must. It is necessary for government, and the diplomats who represent it, and the politicians who lead it, to claim that only they can speak for the whole country. Equally, therefore, they must affirm the nature of the international system by accepting that other governments speak for their whole countries. A modern diplomat would deny that they are so crass as to generalize about other cultures and countries in the way that I have described. Of course, they aver, when they talk about Iran's policy, they mean the policy of the Iranian government, and indeed that is often how they will describe it.

But despite this designative care, the habit of referring to a whole country in the singular and to its government as the embodiment of that state is one as deep-rooted as the state-based international system itself. To change the naming of the actors, to remove the assumption that governments represent the whole of their countries, would be to change the nature of the international system, from one based around states as the primary unit of agency, to one based on some other unit. But as long as governments wish to hold sway in international policy and decision making, they must continually reaffirm not only their own but also others' legitimacy to speak for their countries, even when the government is as grotesquely undemocratic as, say, the Syrian or North Korean regime.

One of the seminal texts that helped define the nature of diplomacy is by François de Callières, published in Paris in 1716.[4] Callières saw the principal function of diplomacy as moderating and managing the clash of conflicting interests as efficiently as possible.

The diplomat was required to assess how the interests of his state, and the other state, could be met in terms acceptable to both.

One can see how remarkably similar this conception of diplomacy is to the way it is usually conceived today. Yet the world is remarkably different. The postwar establishment of new multilateral diplomatic machineries—the United Nations, NATO and the European Union—while creating new forums for state-to-state interactions, has not altered the fundamental idea that diplomacy is about states' identifying their interests and arbitrating them with one another, and that these interests and identities are susceptible to calculation. Indeed, these institutions are premised on the very notion that states can meet there and decide upon their common problems. It is therefore no surprise that diplomats tend to render the world and its myriad problems into these shapes. That this process is becoming more and more artificial, and disconnected from the reality of the forces at work in the world, is only now becoming evident enough to compel change.

The negative consequences of this kind of thinking can be clearly seen in negotiations over issues of common global concern, like climate change. Here, where a shared solution is clearly necessary and urgent, the habit of state-led thinking still dominates. While "world leaders" and UN officials pontificated about the lofty goals of the process, the negotiators in national delegations in the trenches of the conference resorted to type. Zero-sum bargaining over concessions and commitments dominated the discussions, with the usual rancor and finger-pointing when a deal—predictably—proved impossible to find. Some delegates suggested that the Earth's atmosphere was divisible and that the industrialized nations had already taken their "share," as if the atmosphere were a cake to be sliced up.

As the head of Greenpeace dejectedly stated at the dismal end of the Copenhagen summit: "It seems there are too few politicians in this world capable of looking beyond the horizon of their own narrow self-interest, let alone caring much for the millions of people who are facing down the threat of climate change. It is now evident that beating global warming will require a radically different model of politics than the one on display here in Copenhagen." He didn't say what that model was, however.

Some people would argue that the solution to this problem is to increase the number of supranational institutions like the European Union or the United Nations, where unelected officials chosen by the member states can somehow transcend the differences that bedevil nation states.

However, here too the outputs are disappointing. Again, we are confronted with a vast, confusing and obscure tableau of processes and groups and subgroups that pretend to solve common problems, from terrorist financing to avian flu and the Middle East peace process. It is clear that the existence of such processes can have in itself a debilitative effect: The mere existence of a "process" creates the erroneous impression that something is being done, when it is not.

The dysfunctional Copenhagen climate process is one example. Another, lesser known, is the "peace process" to resolve the illegal occupation of the Western Sahara. This "process" has lasted since the cease-fire in 1990 between the occupiers, Morocco, and the representatives of the indigenous people, the Sahrawis—twenty years and counting—when Morocco agreed to a referendum for the territory's people to decide their status, an agreement and legal requirement endorsed many times by the "international community" at the UN. Every country in the world pretends to support this process, run by the UN, but none does anything in reality to advance it. The referendum has never taken place. In fact, the "process" is a way of shelving the issue indefinitely, to permit the existing status quo—of occupation. The process is thus a sham, the opposite of what it pretends to be.

Both the United Nations and the European Union have contributed enormously to limiting the twentieth-century scourge of international conflict. The EU has bound European countries together so tightly that war, once habitual, has now become unthinkable. The UN's sixty-year existence has witnessed a steep decline in the interstate conflict prohibited by its charter. But in these successes, new weaknesses have emerged, not least in dealing with the more fluid and boundaryless problems of the twenty-first century. The UN Security Council was established to prevent wars between states. Today, not less than 80 percent of its agenda concerns issues involving non-state actors, and conflicts both within and sometimes transcending states, like terrorism.[5]

Fatally, all such multilateral or supranational institutions suffer an irredeemable deficit of democratic legitimacy. The greater the distance between representative and elector, the less legitimate that representative. The UN Secretary-General is, at least in theory, supposed to represent us, but no one except the public is expected to believe that he does. The UN Secretary-General is well aware that it is the realpolitikers of the five permanent members of the Security Council who mail his paycheck every month, and he behaves accordingly, just as the president of the EU takes care to keep in close step with the major powers of the EU: France, the UK and Germany. I have often attended meetings between my ambassador at the UN and the Secretary-General where he would be told in unmistakable terms what party line he and his staff were required to toe. It didn't have to be spelled out in threats, merely implied and hinted at. He invariably got the message.

For the ordinary citizen, institutions like the UN and the EU are even more impenetrable and opaque than their already distant national governments. I run a nonprofit diplomatic consultancy. Its staff works full-time to understand the world's diplomatic and multinational institutions, and *we* find it difficult to work out who does what, and where real decisions are made. Pity the ordinary citizen seeking a hearing in the shiny but dismal corridors of the EU's institutions in Brussels. Even for the acute, it is all but impossible to find out who is truly responsible for anything. It is reminiscent of nothing so much as the pathetic queues of provincial Chinese who make desperate but hopeless pilgrimages to Beijing to seek settlement of grievances against corrupt or incompetent Communist Party officials.

Moreover, but more subtly, the officials themselves are dangerously detached from the problem—and the people—they are seeking to arbitrate. I saw this in the UN Security Council—it was a curiously dry and boring place to work despite its dramatic agenda of genocide and civil war. The blood and emotion of these conflicts was absent in its discussions, and it was not a good absence: It was not conducive to better negotiation, but to worse. For one thing, the parties to the disputes on the council's agenda were almost invariably absent from these deliberations—it is hardly a recipe for good decision making to ignore the views of those most concerned. Moreover, the emotional and moral content of events, so crucial to the motivation to solve such problems, was missing. Between the reality of the problems and our deliberations was a huge and unbridgeable divide, not only of actual distance—for we were usually many thousands of miles from the disputes we discussed—but of import.

These deficits are intrinsic to supranational institutions, just as the limits of nation-state thinking are inherent to the nation-state system, a system that has, since the Peace of Westphalia of 1648, dominated world affairs. Given these deficits, the answer to our global problems may not in fact be more diplomacy and international negotiation, at least not of the current kind. Thus conventional wisdom is turned on its head: We do not need more state-to-state diplomacy to solve these problems; we may, in fact, need less. And instead of relying on state-to-state diplomacy to manage the world, we must do so ourselves. As writer Parag Khanna has commented, "As was the case a millennium ago, diplomacy now takes place among anyone who is someone; its prerequisite is not sovereignty but authority."

The deficits of the state-based system are commonly known, yet these systems endure, even when the operators of the system—my many and cynical diplomatic colleagues—have themselves ceased to believe in them. As they take the stand at public inquiries, or address the press, they can hardly believe that anyone still believes them. It is a hollow, hollow feeling and I know it. These systems will continue to endure until those in whose name they claim to function withdraw their consent. The pact is broken; it doesn't work. To name a problem as "international" is to absolve oneself of responsibility and to place a solution in the hands of those proven manifestly incapable. The international is not international anymore; it is simply us.

And here is the most insidious and yet hidden effect of the international system—of interstate diplomacy—as it currently exists. It is not that this system may exacerbate differences, force its players to define themselves more starkly than they otherwise might, nor that its exponents must naturally reflect a calculus not of the messy and diverse human family but of these strange and artificial units, states, or that these exponents are, as I once was, wholly separated from their sense of moral responsibility for their actions. These deficits are not the worst aspect of this system. (The "Live 8" text messages to the G8 Summit provide a clue.)

The most dangerous effect of the system is not that it doesn't work; it is that we, in whose name it is supposed to function, condone it, pretend to believe it contrary to all evidence and permit it to continue.*

It is one thing to accept this critique, but it is another to embody this philosophical shift. In a world of global terrorism, a rising India and China, and intense national competition for scarce resources, what meaningful action is available to the individual? How can the world be made to reflect its human reality rather than its inherited and inappropriate delineations of segregated states and peoples?

One obvious answer is for individuals to organize across nations and states around common causes. This is already beginning to happen: Witness the global movements around climate change or the protection of human rights. (Ideas to guide such action will be elaborated later.) Less encouragingly, such borderless cooperation is also visible in the transnational organization of drug trafficking or jihadist terrorism, where extremists of many different nationalities have gathered around the flag of the new Umma.

IT IS TOO EASY to succumb to defeatism in regarding the world today—its weapons, its states, its self-serving and bumptious leaders. How on earth are we supposed to deal with that? It might be revealing to look at an issue that inspires the most pessimism and also the

---

*These arguments are more fully discussed in my earlier book *Independent Diplomat: Dispatches from an Unaccountable Elite.*

most horror. Nuclear weapons embody in their very existence the possibility of appalling destruction and indeed the annihilation of humanity as a species. In some ways, they manifest the gross inhumanity of the state system—that in order to defend the state, governments are prepared to use weapons that threaten the destruction not only of their own population, but of the entire world's.

The conventional answer to this problem has been to look to governments to get rid of nuclear weapons. Even the demonstrators massing on the streets waving banners ultimately urge their governments to respond. Is this a realistic ambition?

The 2010 review conference of the Non-Proliferation Treaty (NPT), the cornerstone of the world's efforts to reduce nuclear weapons, lasted a month and involved highly skilled delegations from some one hundred ninety countries. The agreement they reached was lauded as a success, primarily because, unlike previous review conferences for the last decade, this gathering had actually achieved agreement. But the content of the agreement—the *output*—was feeble, despite the international atmosphere being its most propitious for decades.

As usual, the "outcome document" was long—twenty-eight jargon-laden and barely comprehensible pages—with a misleading sixty-four "action points," most of which amounted to no substantive action whatsoever. The vast majority were declarative: "reaffirming," "welcoming" or "noting." The press, focusing on one small part of the forest, made great play of the agreement to hold a conference—in the future—on a nuclear-free Middle East, but even that agreement left out the only country in the Middle East currently possessing nuclear weapons, Israel. Otherwise, the conference agreed merely to *encourage* the nuclear weapons states to make more concrete progress toward nuclear disarmament and reduce the use of nuclear weapons in their military doctrines; but attempts to make such disarmament concrete and obligatory through a nuclear weapons convention were fiercely resisted by the nuclear weapons states. As even the most favorable commentators put it, all that was agreed was a further *process*, not an output.[6]

In its closing statement, Cuba noted pointedly what the review conference had *not* agreed to: no timetable on nuclear disarmament; no commitment to begin negotiations on a nuclear weapons convention; no clear commitment to stop the development of nuclear weapons; no call for withdrawal of nuclear weapons to home territories (i.e., out of Europe); and no legally binding negative security assurances—we shall come to these strange creatures later.

President Obama has declared his intention of ultimately ridding the world of nuclear weapons. The Global Zero campaign, supported by many prominent former statesmen and women and highlighted in a popular documentary film, *Countdown to Zero*, is advocating the same. But it is a fair bet that in the current state-based dispensation, these noble efforts will fail. For it is implausible to expect that China, or Russia, or even France or Britain, let alone Israel or Pakistan, will give up this ultimate guarantor of their security, even if some reductions may nevertheless be possible. As total arsenals go down, louder and louder will become the argument that nuclear weapons have successfully prevented mass conventional war between their possessors. It's a plausible argument, as long as the proxy conventional wars that these powers fought on the territories of others are ignored. But nonetheless, the argument has force. Total disarmament relies on something that evidently does not exist—complete confidence and trust in the commitments of others that they too have disarmed irreversibly, and that they will not launch conventional attack.

The NPT's answer to this problem is fundamentally ridiculous.

To the non-nuclear states who demand assurance that they will not be the victim of nuclear attack, the nuclear weapons states (NWS) have offered "reverse security guarantees"—promises that they will not use nuclear weapons against non-nuclear states in certain circumstances. The "progress" of the 2010 review conference was that the conference agreed to *consider* making these "guarantees" legally binding. In other words, if a nuclear weapons state dropped the bomb or bombs on a non-nuclear state, the victim state would be able to seek redress in an international court, presuming that there would remain—post-apocalypse—a government, lawyers or courts with which to press such a claim. And such legal obligations would arise only if the nuclear weapons states agree to them, which they have yet to do: At the review conference, they agreed only to "consider" them. Such reverse guarantees, even if legally enforceable, are unlikely to provide much reassurance if, for instance, Ukraine finds itself dealing with a fascist-led nuclear-armed Russia, which unfortunately is a more plausible prospect than the legally binding reverse security assurances.

Under the NPT, the UK, like all other declared nuclear-armed states, is in theory committed to disarm itself of all of its nuclear weapons. The NPT was founded on a conceptual bargain—that the rest of the countries of the world would not develop their own nuclear weapons capability, as long as the nuclear weapons states agreed to get rid of theirs eventually. One indicator of the "progress" made at the 2010 conference was that the UK for the first time declared the full number of its nuclear weapons. No other declared NWS has done so. Revealingly but perhaps also most honestly, France insisted that the goal of the NPT "process" be stated not as a "world free of nuclear weapons," but as the creation of "conditions which will lead to a world free of nuclear weapons."

Earlier that year, the U.S. and Russia agreed under the Strategic
Arms Reduction Treaty, or START, to a reduction in their arsenals of
nuclear weapons. Heralded as offering substantial new reductions,
some analysts judge that in reality the agreement barely affects the
number of actual deployed weapons, and involves no reduction in
the number of Russian launch vehicles.[7] Both powers continue to
maintain hundreds of nuclear delivery systems at Cold War levels
of alert: ready to be launched within a few minutes. One respected
think tank noted that "while the operational readiness of some weapon
systems has been reduced, there has been no major change in the
readiness levels of most of the nuclear weapon systems in the post–
Cold War era."[8]

Instead, it is more plausible to refer to, reinforce and promote a
reality that the diplomats, politicians and analysts refuse to contemplate. The calculus of nuclear weapons depends upon the existence
of the chessboard—a "Them" and an "Us." If you attack me, I will
attack you: black and white pieces, segregated and discrete. If those
distinctions no longer exist, the game cannot be played. Instead of
two distinct sets of pawns and pieces, clearly separated across the
board, all pieces are but varying shades of gray, intermingled and
spread all over the board. This depiction is much closer to the contemporary reality, and the more time passes, the more accurate it will
become. A Pakistani attack on New Delhi would kill hundreds of
thousands of Muslims. An attack on Israel would kill thousands
of Arabs. Any use of nuclear weapons, more or less anywhere, would
have devastating effects on a highly interlinked global economy. Destroying New York would kill people from every country on earth.
People of more than ninety nationalities were killed in the destruction of the twin towers; one borough of the city contains at least 160
different nationalities. Killing Them would mean killing Us.

Nuclear weapons make this doubly true as even a limited strike on one country would, according to recent research, imply appalling consequences for the whole planet. Studies have shown that even a "small-scale" nuclear exchange, say, India and Pakistan launching fifty weapons each against each other, would have devastating consequences not only for the countries directly targeted but also for the global environment and potentially for the survival of mankind.[9] Thus, nuclear weapons are revealed in their true nature: not as weapons of deterrence or plausible utility, but as mankind's suicide pill.

This truth is already slowly spreading among some enlightened members of the military, who are realizing that the use of nuclear weapons by states is basically implausible—and self-destructive—in almost any circumstance. The most likely people to use nuclear weapons are not states but suicidal millenarian terrorists. Osama bin Laden's deputy Ayman al-Zawahiri has already written a book dismissing moral objections to the use of weapons of mass destruction, including nuclear weapons.[10] Our possession of nuclear weapons is no deterrent to such threats, but the very existence of nuclear weapons provides a possible method for these extremists. Thus, the best thing would be to do away with them altogether.

Establish this as a cultural truth, and eventually that understanding will filter through. Wherever possible, travel, interact, make love, argue, live with people elsewhere. Engage; co-mingle. Resist the efforts of governments and others to paint the Other in stark colors, whether black or white. Throw away the chessboard; cut the ground from under those who would pretend humanity is but chessmen. Cease using the outdated nomenclature of a world that is already receding into history; stop naming; stop dividing.

One surprising conclusion from this analysis might come as a shock to the antiglobalization protesters storming the next G8 Summit: What might be the most effective tactic ultimately to get rid of nuclear weapons is not less globalization, but *more*. The deeper the intermingling, the more dense the mesh connecting humanity, the less the chessboard may be clearly defined, the more absurd becomes the calculus of nuclear weapons, and indeed of states as discrete entities, themselves.

Interestingly, this reasoning also applies to other harmful, if less apocalyptic, forms of warfare. Many have expressed concern that China or Russia is able to launch devastating "cyber attacks" against Western institutions, and economic and financial infrastructure. But one Chinese official has reportedly dismissed this option, primarily on the grounds of China's dependence on U.S. financial stability: China owns nearly a trillion dollars' worth of securitized American government debt—a cyber attack on Wall Street would harm China as much as it harmed the U.S.[11]

These examples suggest that the antiglobalizers storming the G8-protecting riot police are precisely wrong.

Instead of conventional theories of government and international relations, we need a new set of tools—and perhaps a dose of humility too, for a complex world may defy all but a general understanding of its inherent and pervasive unpredictability and contingency. In fact, we need the tools that interpret complex systems.

Malcolm Gladwell has popularized the concept of the "tipping point," the idea from complexity theory that even small events may trigger complex systems to "tip" over from one condition into another. Historian Niall Ferguson and others have begun to suggest that empires, such as the American "empire," are complex systems and thus may be highly vulnerable to outside events, perhaps seemingly minor, over which they have little or no control, causing their downfall.[12] In finance, Nassim Nicholas Taleb has suggested that highly aberrational "black swan" events, hitherto regarded as extremely rare, are in reality much more frequent than predicted, and moreover have vastly more dramatic consequences. The May 2010 "flash crash" on the Dow Jones seemed to prove his point.

There is, then, a growing realization that human affairs make up in their totality a complex system. Complex systems share characteristics which have important but barely noted consequences for politics.

Complex systems are *not* chaotic. They are not simple and ordered, but neither are they an uncontrolled mess. Complex systems are instead something "in between," as Professor Scott Page, an expert on complexity, has observed.[13]

Another characteristic is perhaps the most telling, and recollects the stadium wave or the suicide bomber. The actions of one individual may redound in very powerful and consequential ways. This insight is a conclusion completely at odds with contemporary notions of the ranking and power of government, state and individual. The individual is not powerless, not subordinate; in fact individuals are a potent agent of lasting change in the whole system.

If individuals begin to behave in the way suggested in this book—to act themselves to produce desired political results, cooperating and negotiating directly with others affected—then a new dispensation will emerge, something that we may not yet be able to describe. This is the phenomenon of "emergence," a key characteristic of complexity: that from the combined actions of many agents, acting according to their own microcosmic preferences and values, a new condition may emerge from the bottom up, almost unconsciously, and certainly without imposition by government, god or anyone else.

INTELLECTUALLY, we understand that turning a vast heterogeneous mesh into a chessboard of discrete players is to do something inherently reductive, oversimplifying and thus, in its way, deceptive if not downright dishonest. It is simply not possible credibly to claim that any authority, like any historian, can understand this huge pattern of interaction and connection. They cannot know, yet they must claim to.

But there is something still more insidious going on. In claiming authority to organize our affairs, to order the Pollock-like mélange into something that it isn't, governments take away something more crucial from us—our own agency. Or rather, they take away our own *sense* of agency, for in truth our control over events never left us, only our belief in its existence.

Contrary to common assumptions, individuals acting collectively have a far greater power to control their circumstances, and indeed those of the whole world, than governments pretend. The immediate overthrow of governments now would bring only chaos. But as individuals and groups begin to assert their own agency over decisions and events within their own reach, there will eventually emerge a much wider and more fundamental effect, one that would ultimately amount to a revolution in how we organize our affairs.

How this might look is inherently unpredictable. No one can know how the sum of such deliberate actions might appear. This is, above all, a cultural change not an architectural redesign of political structures. Gustav Landauer, a nineteenth-century theorist, once wrote:

> The state is not something which can be destroyed by a revolution,
> but is a condition, a certain relationship between human beings, a

mode of human behavior; we destroy it by contracting other relationships, by behaving differently.

It will start with individuals acting upon their convictions. It will continue and gather force as they join together—perhaps in person, perhaps on the Web—to organize, not to campaign, but to *act* and embody the changes they seek. These networks of cooperation may be temporary; they may be long-lasting. They may encompass a street, or the inhabitants of a building, cooperating to manage their affairs. They may span the globe as millions act together to address a shared concern. The embryonic forms of such cooperation are already evident: There are consumer cooperatives that bargain for lower prices; "common security clubs" where unemployed people share job-seeking skills, barter services and organize shared childcare;[14] local groups where unemployed handymen and babysitters offer their services to the community;[15] and Internet campaigns that enroll millions across the globe.

As the realization of governments' dwindling power spreads, this new form of politics will become less about protest or petition and more about action. The sum of these collectives will not have a fixed structure; they will ebb and flow, responsive to the changing needs and passions of the population. They may be local, but they will also transcend borders, inevitably weakening the mental hold of boundaries and inherited national identities upon peoples with common interests. One day, so strong may be this new culture of collective collaboration, and this mesh of different networks of cooperation, that our existing institutions, based on the singularizing, centralizing unit of national government, and indeed the notion of the nation state, may wither away, unneeded, outdated, irrelevant.

This mesh of networks, of collaborating groups both local and transnational, represents in its indefinite shapes its dynamic changing nature and its responsiveness to the needs of its participants—us, ordinary people—a form much closer to the actual nature of the world today, its diverse and massive flows, the multiplying and shifting identities of its peoples, and above all its manifold challenges. And in its consonance with the nature of the world, that mesh, that shape—indeterminate, unstructured, changing though it may be—offers paradoxically much greater stability and coherence than the fixed and hierarchical forms of organization we have inherited from the past. The world should be ordered according to our needs, not the projections and requirements of static institutions.

The future nature of this world cannot be foreseen; it will *emerge*. But one thing is sure. No longer would we be fooled into seeing the world as a chessboard, demarcated, separated, neat, but instead it would seem to us as it really is.

7

THE MEANS ARE THE ENDS

I n colonial India, the British forbade Indians to make their own salt, and charged steeply for it as a form of indirect taxation on the subject people, a tax that hit the poorest especially hard. In 1930, Mahatma Gandhi decided to attack this injustice directly, and organized a march to India's coast, where salt could be made from seawater—for free—directly challenging the British monopoly of salt production. Gandhi's "Salt Satyagraha," or "Salt March," is rightly renowned as one of the most important acts of political protest in recent history.

Gandhi chose to attack the salt tax, against the advice of some of his political colleagues, because it was both a tool and a symbol of Britain's oppression. Thus, the action to undermine the tax assumed both a practical and symbolic value. Gandhi carefully planned the march, choosing only his most disciplined cohorts from his own ashram, and sending scouts to reconnoiter villages ahead. He built up public expectations and attention with press conferences before and during the march. The Salt March above all manifested a core principle of Gandhi's political philosophy—that of *satyagraha*—a synthesis of the Sanskrit words *satya* (truth) and *agraha* (holding firmly). In the common shorthand of today's times, Gandhi's philosophy is often summarized as "nonviolence" or "passive resistance," and indeed it encompasses these elements. But for Gandhi, *satyagraha* had a deeper and more positive significance, not merely an absence of violence but more a strength. In his words:

> Truth (satya) implies love, and firmness (agraha) engenders and therefore serves as a synonym for force. I thus began to call the Indian movement Satyagraha, that is to say, the Force which is born of Truth and Love or nonviolence, and gave up the use of the phrase "passive resistance," in connection with it, so much so that even in English writing we often avoided it and used instead the word "satyagraha."[1]

Above all, Gandhi believed that means were intimately connected with ends. Indeed, they were to him the same thing, as connected as a tree to its seed. If you used violence, you could expect nothing but further violence in return. *Satyagraha* by contrast engaged a force—love—to which there was no resistance. The Salt March demonstrated clearly how these concepts, combined with an acute political intelligence, played out in practice.

The British, at first dismissive, were confused as to how to respond to the march, which gained huge publicity in India and worldwide. It was reported that sixty thousand Indians came to hear Gandhi speak on the eve of the march. Not one to eschew melodrama, Gandhi warned that his speech might be the last words of his life; he invoked a compelling spirit of self-sacrifice: "My task shall be done if I perish and so do my comrades." As the march progressed, crowds of tens and sometimes hundreds of thousands gathered along the way. Gandhi's marchers slept in the open in the villages they passed through, asking for only food and water, the better, Gandhi judged, to recruit India's poor, whose support would be vital to imperialism's defeat.

After a march lasting nearly three weeks and nearly two hundred fifty miles, building up expectations and political tension all the way, Gandhi arrived at the coastal village of Dandi in Gujarat, where raising a handful of mud which he then boiled to make salt, Gandhi declared, "With this, I am shaking the foundations of the British Empire." Gandhi implored his followers and all Indians to follow his example and make illegal salt, breaking the British monopoly and depriving the empire of an important source of revenue. In the weeks that followed, sixty thousand people were arrested for making salt. At Peshawar, British troops killed over two hundred peaceful demonstrators. Gandhi was arrested while planning his next *satyagraha* at the Dharasana salt works. The march went ahead, eventually under the leadership of Sarojini Naidu, a female poet and freedom fighter. She warned her fellow Satyagrahis to expect to be beaten, but that "you must not even raise a hand to fend off blows." Sure enough, soldiers beat the marchers with steel-tipped clubs. As United Press reported:

> Not one of the marchers even raised an arm to fend off the blows. They went down like ten-pins. From where I stood I heard the sickening whacks of the clubs on unprotected skulls. The waiting crowd of watchers groaned and sucked in their breaths in sympathetic pain at every blow. Those struck down fell sprawling, unconscious or

writhing in pain with fractured skulls or broken shoulders. In two
or three minutes the ground was quilted with bodies. Great patches
of blood widened on their white clothes. The survivors without
breaking ranks silently and doggedly marched on until struck down.[2]

Despite its receiving worldwide attention, this sacrifice failed to
win any immediate concessions from the British, and it would be
another seventeen years before India would at last be independent.
Though India's first prime minister, Jawaharlal Nehru, acknowledged
the enormous importance of the Salt March in mobilizing India's
masses around the goal of independence, his Congress Party, to which
Gandhi then belonged, eventually abandoned *satyagraha* as a political technique. Historians today tend to view the Second World War
as the more significant factor in ending imperial rule in India.[3] But
the Salt Satyagraha is remembered still for its signal achievement
in one crucial aspect. As one British colonial administrator noted
at the time, "England can hold India only by consent; we can't rule
it by the sword." And thanks to the Salt March, they had lost that
consent.

Though technically the more powerful of the two antagonists—
with the power of the state, of arrest and ultimately of force—Britain
lost the contest against Gandhi's force of will, *satyagraha*. Those who
were clubbed to the ground ended up victorious, for by their reaction
to the march, the British lost the consent of the Indian population,
upon which they relied to maintain their colonial rule. The Salt
Satyagraha thus qualifies as one of the most effective political actions
of recent times. It is worth summarizing why:

- It confronted its political target—Britain's colonial rule—
  directly: The goal of the Salt March was to make salt, directly

confronting the British salt tax and denying the colonialists revenue; thus the action itself contributed to the political result intended.

- Its nonviolent methods confounded and confused the British; a British administrator later confessed in an internal memo that the British would have preferred violence.
- By combining means and ends nonviolently, the march attracted and created enormous moral force, which not only helped recruit followers but was also crucial in garnering massive international attention and sympathy.

In an age of terrorism and violent counterreaction, such examples can seem quaint and irrelevant, but surveys suggest that even in the Muslim world, Al Qaeda's use of violence, and in particular its targeting of civilians, alienates more followers than it attracts. The persuasive power of self-sacrifice and nonviolence remains undiminished, even if violence seems once again the more fashionable.

In his short manual *Guerrilla Warfare*, Che Guevara dismisses terrorist violence as ineffective:

> We sincerely believe that terrorism is of negative value, that it by no means produces the desired effects, that it can turn a people against a revolutionary movement, and that it can bring a loss of lives to its agents out of proportion to what it produces.[4]

Guevara preferred direct military confrontation with the repressive forces of Batista, Cuba's then dictator. In modern Mexico, recognizing that conditions, though unjust, were less repressive than in pre-revolutionary Cuba, the leader of the Zapatista rebels in Mexico's Chiapas region, Subcomandante Marcos, prefers irony and nonviolence to bring home the Zapatistas' message of the exploitation of Mexico's indigenous peoples. As Marcos put it:

> We don't want to impose our solutions by force, we want to create a democratic space. We don't see armed struggle in the classic sense of previous guerrilla wars, that is as the only way and the only all-powerful truth around which everything is organized. In a war, the decisive thing is not the military confrontation but the politics at stake in the confrontation. We didn't go to war to kill or be killed. We went to war in order to be heard.[5]

Gandhi himself sometimes despaired of the Indian people's propensity for violence. Exploiting his immense public standing and moral authority, on several occasions he used hunger strikes as a tool of political persuasion, including to seek an end to fighting between Muslims and Hindus.

This technique too has modern relevance. The hunger strikes by Republican inmates in the Maze prison in Northern Ireland in 1981 resulted in the deaths of several strikers, most famously Bobby Sands, who was elected as a member of the British Parliament during his hunger strike. After ten inmates died, the British government offered some concessions. The most lasting impact, however, was, like the Salt Satyagraha, deeper in its effects on that intangible: will. By 1985, the British government had negotiated the Anglo-Irish agreement that gave the Irish Republic for the first time a consultative role in the government of Northern Ireland, and heralded the peace process that resulted in the Good Friday agreement of 1998, which largely brought an end, though sadly not yet final, to the violence and sectarian strife that had benighted the province for over thirty years.

In 2009, a forty-two-year-old woman named Aminatou Haidar

used the hunger strike for similar effect. A native of the Western Sahara, which has been occupied by Morocco since 1975, Haidar has ceaselessly campaigned for the right of her people, the Sahrawi, to self-determination.[6] For these efforts, she has been repeatedly imprisoned and abused. Returning from the United States, where she had been awarded various human rights prizes, Haidar was prevented by Morocco from reentering the territory where she and her children live. The Moroccans seized her passport and demanded she sign an oath of allegiance to Morocco's king in order to get it back. She refused and went on a hunger strike to demand its return. As Haidar approached death, international efforts on her behalf stepped up and even Morocco's allies, France and the United States, were forced to intervene. After thirty-two days without food, Haidar was taken to the hospital, her respiration and blood pressure dangerously low. She remained, however, committed to the end, determined, she said, to return unimpeded and without conditions or to die in dignity. Morocco at last capitulated and permitted her return, a public humiliation for a monarchy that had sworn it would not back down. Thanks to her willingness to starve herself to the end, Haidar not only secured her own return to her homeland, but also succeeded in attracting unprecedented international attention to Morocco's occupation of Africa's "last colony."

Sometimes protest can take the simplest form. In East Timor, then occupied by Indonesia, the indigenous East Timorese would approach every Indonesian soldier or settler they came across and ask, "When are you leaving my country?"[7] The most basic declaration of discontent, repeated, sends a signal that the status quo cannot endure.

In the summer of 1964, about a thousand American students mainly from northern colleges—most of them white—traveled to

Mississippi as part of a campaign by the Student Nonviolent Co-ordinating Committee (SNCC) to fight against racial segregation in the southern states. The students lived in communes—"Freedom Houses"—or with local black families. They registered voters and taught in Freedom Schools. In one of the most notorious crimes of the civil rights era, three recently arrived students were beaten to death by segregationists assisted by the local police, killings made famous in the movie *Mississippi Burning*. The murders shocked the world. As with Claudette Colvin, who refused to change seats on her bus, the students' actions directly contributed to the repeal of the notorious racist Jim Crow laws and the end of legalized segregation in the South, a reminder that laws follow action, not vice versa.

These dramatic actions were often taken to address grave injustices, like occupation and systematic repression. The hunger strike is an extreme action taken in response to extreme circumstances. Moreover, as Gandhi and Haidar both illustrate, it helps that the striker already enjoys some standing in public, and ideally, as in both cases, moral authority.

Political actions which produce, even in small part, the political end they seek carry a persuasive force far greater than any mere campaign, both for their demonstrative and symbolic force, and for the simple reason that such actions, even if only on a small scale, contribute to the desired solution.

For example, in New York City's Bedford-Stuyvesant, after a spate of robberies, a group of local men decided to escort pedestrians home from the subway. One of the founders of "We Make Us Better" said, "I decided we can't have these people terrorizing our young women and children, and we're not speaking up and making our presence felt." The members of the group don't regard themselves as political or activist; they are just trying to make their community better by their example.[8] They plan soon to set up a mentoring program.

This illustrates an important message—that it is changing attitudes and demonstrating new forms of behavior, as much as laws, that matters. This lesson is also evident in Naples, the heartland of the Camorra organized crime ring. Here, local people have taken the initiative to resist extortion and corruption, some pasting "anti-*pizzo*" stickers on their shops to indicate that they do not pay protection money, and as a signal of solidarity with those who do the same. Others are establishing cooperatives to run the farms and businesses seized by prosecutors from the mafia.

IN A COUNTRY where several legislators and the prime minister are accused of links to the mob, a judge made the same point, "The battle is not just won by force and sequestrations, but by a social struggle. It is a cultural battle."[9]

In Britain, Prime Minister David Cameron has made great play of a concept he calls "The Big Society," offering a rather sketchy blend of a vague localism with more familiar Conservative moral philosophy about individual responsibility. At the same time that the government has made severe cuts in public spending, Cameron has argued that people should play a greater role in local activities, hitherto the preserve of government, including schools, parks and other public services. The conjunction of cuts with the moral sermonizing is not the only aspect of the Big Society that jars. This book argues that people will benefit by taking charge of their shared affairs locally, but crucially this means that they must also have *agency* over these decisions: control. The benefits outlined here—of better and more equitable outcomes, and social consensus, from local and participatory decision-making—are not available in the Big Society, because in Cameron's vision central government retains overall control. If taxes and revenues are collected and distributed centrally, it is impossible for people at the local level to have real control over budgets and thus policy.

The Porto Alegre experiment described earlier is an example of what real local agency looks like, and its benefits are clear—above all in the more equitable distribution of government services, but also in greater social consensus underpinning policy choices. The Big Society, by contrast, has yet to amount to real autonomy at the local level. Local people may provide, but not decide. It is this contradiction that perhaps explains Cameron's inability to explain his concept with any clarity, and suggests that it will amount to little more than encouraging volunteers at the local library. For this half-baked philosophy entirely misses the point of real devolution of power. Indeed, it represents no such devolution in substantive terms at all. All that it offers is responsibility without power.

In 1980, CEOs of the largest American companies earned an average of forty-two times as much as the average worker; in 2001, they earned 531 times as much. It is hard to imagine that these bosses have in twenty years increased their contribution to company performance by such a remarkable degree. Instead, there appears to be an emerging culture among the top executives that, because they *can* pay themselves so much, they should. This self-interested belief piggybacks upon and exploits a vague cultural notion that competitive economies somehow *require* exceptional rewards for the successful. Thus capitalism takes on not only the qualities of an economic system, but also a moral code.

There is nothing inevitable about such excesses, or inequality. Such irresponsible greed is not necessary for a competitive company, nor intrinsic to an efficient economy. Indeed, the opposite seems to be the case. Some economists, including a former International Monetary Fund chief economist, now believe that America's gross wealth inequality lay at the root of the financial meltdown: Middle-class families, whose incomes have been stagnant for a decade, were forced to borrow more and more to buy houses and maintain acceptable living standards.[10] Meanwhile, the rich, who enjoyed a far greater share of the rewards of America's economic growth over the last decade, spend far less as a proportion of their overall income, depressing the consumption necessary to fuel sustained growth.*

But what might be done?

John Lewis set up his first draper's shop in 1864. His son Spedan joined the business toward the end of the century. While convalescing from a riding accident, he realized that his father, his brother and he together earned more than all the hundreds of other employees in the family's two stores put together. Spedan Lewis instigated new systems and practices as soon as he returned to work: He offered shortened working days, set up a staff committee, and a third week's paid holiday, an innovation for retail trade at the time. He founded a house magazine, *The Gazette*, which is still published today.

---

*By economist Raghuram Rajan's calculations, "from every dollar of growth in income between 1976 and 2007, 58 cents went to the top 1% of households. The other 99% of American families had to scrap over the 42 cents of loose change. The result was a country as unequal as it had been just before the Wall Street crash of 1929—and with much the same results." Aditya Chakrabortty, "What the £35,000 Cocktail Taught Us," *The Guardian*, August 2, 2010.

In 1920, Spedan introduced a profit-sharing scheme. Twenty years later, it was expanded into a partnership: In effect, Lewis handed over the business to its workers. Today, nearly seventy thousand partner employees own the scores of major stores and supermarkets operated by John Lewis across Britain. Every branch holds forums to discuss local issues. These aggregate to form divisional councils; partners elect the large majority of members of the Partnership Council. The councils have the power to discuss "any issue whatsoever"; the partnership puts "the happiness of Partners at the centre of everything it does."

The partnership's constitution sets out to be both commercial and democratic. The annual bonus for partners in 2008 was equivalent to ten weeks' wages. The partners own two country estates, sailing clubs, golf courses, hotels and other extensive recreational and social facilities. Pension schemes are generous; after twenty-five years' service partners are rewarded with six months' paid leave. With its well-known slogan of "Never knowingly undersold" and a guarantee that it will repay customers the difference if they can find a lower price elsewhere (though not online), John Lewis has been consistently profitable, despite the cutthroat competition of the retail sector. Its revenues in 2008 were nearly £7 billion.

Speaking in 1963, shortly before he died, Spedan Lewis explained why he set up the partnership and handed over what had been the family business to its employees.

> It was soon clear to me that my father's success had been due to his trying constantly to give very good value to people who wished to exchange their money for his merchandise but it also became clear to me that the business would have grown further and that my father's life would have been much happier if he had done the same for those who wished to exchange their work for his money.

The profit . . . was equal to the whole of the pay of the staff, of whom there were about three hundred. To his two children my father seemed to have all that anyone could want. Yet for years he had been spending no more than a small fraction of his income.

On the other hand, for very nearly all of his staff any saving worth mentioning was impossible. They were getting hardly more than a bare living. The pay-sheet was small even for those days.[11]

Note that Lewis suggests that his father would have been happier himself if he had paid his workers more fairly, an observation borne out in the 2009 book *The Spirit Level*, by Richard Wilkinson and Kate Pickett (Penguin), which found that everyone in society is better off—in terms of mental health, crime and other indicators—in economies with greater wealth equality. Spedan Lewis continued that the state of affairs in the country was a "perversion of capitalism":

It is all wrong to have millionaires before you have ceased to have slums. Capitalism has done enormous good and suits human nature far too well to be given up as long as human nature remains the same. But the perversion has given us too unstable a society. Differences of reward must be large enough to induce people to do their best but the present differences are far too great. If we do not find some way of correcting that perversion of capitalism, our society will break down. We shall find ourselves back in some form of government without the consent of the governed, some form of police state.

Cooperative businesses, such as John Lewis and Spain's Mondragon, which pays its executives no more than eight times its lowest paid employees, have shown that businesses owned by their employees can be as successful as the most hierarchical, profit-driven enterprise. At such companies, wage differentials are lower, benefits are more widely shared, and above all, employees who are also owners feel not only more agency over the future of their business, and thus their own future, but also more satisfaction. These companies are not compelled to a more egalitarian approach by legislation; they were set up that way by the free choice of their founders.

Founded in 1884 by Karl Eisener, who wanted to provide long-term jobs to discourage the Swiss from emigrating because of poor economic conditions, the knife company Victorinox is going strong, with a respected global brand nearly a hundred twenty years later.[12] Still, it suffered a severe crisis when penknives were banned from airports, hitherto important sales channels, under post-9/11 airport security measures. The company responded by referring to its values of inclusiveness and loyalty to its workers. Despite a steep decline in sales, no one was laid off. The company instead stopped hiring, encouraged workers to take early vacations and reduced shifts, while expanding its product ranges, particularly in watches. The company had suffered similar crises before, such as a sharp decrease in orders from the Swiss army after the First World War.

Victorinox, in contrast to the prevailing hire-and-fire model, treats its workers the same, in good times as well as bad. It acts according to its pronounced values (means and ends again) by establishing employee-oriented management schemes and an integration policy that better incorporates younger and older workers, immigrants and people with disabilities. It pays the highest-paid workers no more than five times the wages of the average.

In the financial sector, mutual banks and insurance companies endured the depredations of the financial crisis much better than publicly owned banks and companies. Mutuals, by their very nature, discourage excessive risk-taking and indeed excessive pay. They return banks to the old-fashioned notion that lending should not grossly outpace deposits. The trouble is that stock-market listing encourages the emphasis on short-term profits—and thus risk-taking—that contributed to such problems in the credit crunch. The ensuing government bailout of the banks reaffirmed the implicit guarantee that no major bank would be allowed to fail and risk wider economic meltdown. Thus, the current system, even after the much-heralded "bill to control Wall Street" in 2009, and thanks to government action, rewards the most destructive Wall Street behavior.

Boston University professor Laurence Kotlikoff has proposed that all financial products be mutualized as "limited-purpose banking" (LPB) with benefits in reduced risk, greater transparency and less excessive executive compensation. Under LPB, mortgage lending, for example, would take place through "mortgage mutual funds" whose managers would pick loans to invest in. Mortgage applicants would provide the information they do today, and different funds could bid for their custom. The lenders would be investors owning shares in the mutual funds. At no point would any bank actually hold the mortgage on its books. Indeed, banks would not hold anything on their books at all except the modest assets needed to manage a fund—computers and offices—and the matching equity. They would neither borrow nor trade with borrowed funds. Kotlikoff extends this principle to all of finance, including insurance and derivatives. His proposed system, crucially, would mean that all contingent liabilities would be fully backed by capital.[13]

In defending the inequities and excesses of the current system, the beneficiaries of these injustices tout half-baked economic arguments remarkably often, such as the economic necessity of enormous executive "compensation." In public debate, the merits of private enterprise are invariably presented as superior to government provision. These arguments come to a head over "public goods" such as the nation's health or the world's oceans, where the choice is usually presented as between private ownership or public provision and regulation: market versus the state. Evident in these debates is an assumption that there are only two options—public or private—to resolve the "tragedy of the commons," whereby common resources such as water, land or oceans will be abused by some, and neglected by all, without some form of order.

In fact, pioneering economists have shown that other spontaneous forms of voluntary management and sharing of such resources have sprung up and are, if anything, more successful at husbanding these common goods than either of the two conventional models. One such economist was awarded the Nobel Prize for economics in 2009. Professor Elinor Ostrom's work has shown that societies and groups regularly devise rules and enforcement mechanisms that stop the degradation of nature. The traditional theory holds that pollution and depletion of resources would occur because individuals fail to recognize—or do not care about—their effect on others. However, her research has shown that people can manage resources tolerably well without rules imposed by the authorities if rules evolved over time, entitlements were clear, conflict resolution measures were available and an individual's duty to maintain the common resource was in proportion to the benefits from exploiting it. Notably, she found that the most important criterion for the success of such schemes was this: active participation in setting and enforcing the collective rules to manage the common good.[14]

The tortured debate over health care illustrates this problem. In the U.S., a system dominated by massive private insurance companies has created enormous and escalating costs for American business and many other distortions and inequities, particularly for the poor, who have been excluded from private insurance provision. Vast sums may be spent to prolong the lives of the well-insured for merely a few days, while many millions of the poor endure chronic or even fatal illness without treatment. Ideologues from the right, but also the heavily lobbied representatives of both Democrats and Republicans, successfully destroyed the "public option"—that government should provide insurance—in the 2009 health care bill. Needless to say, the enormous health insurance industry spent over $600 million on lobbying in the two years before the bill.

Meanwhile, in the UK, where public provision—and universal coverage—of health care is entrenched in the form of the National Health Service, there is very appropriate concern, among both doctors and patients, at the overweening and barely accountable bureaucracy seemingly necessary to run the system, and the sometimes arbitrary choices it must make, for instance, that certain drugs be denied to the sick because they are too expensive.

In both countries, the fundamental truth of any health care system, whether public or private, is barely acknowledged—that there must be some system of rationing care. Otherwise, demand for health care is insatiable; its costs would eventually consume the entire economy, as the costs of America's insurance-based system indeed threaten to do if unchecked.

Arrangements to include both doctors and patients equally in the provision of health care have worked in the past, and work today. In earlier eras, cooperative or "friendly" societies pooled the contributions of working families to provide care when illness or death struck. Today, health care cooperatives are able successfully to manage and deploy their available resources according to what their members (i.e., patients)—and not the insurance companies or bureaucrats—regard as important. This possibility is barely mentioned in the U.S.

debate, presumably because cooperatives have no lobbyists. If it does arise, the idea of cooperatives is often hysterically attacked by both the insurance industry, which claims cooperatives are public provision in disguise, or by advocates for the "public option," who argue that nonprofits cannot possibly compete with the massive cartels of the insurance giants. Neither argument stands up to scrutiny, for cooperatives would operate without taxpayer support, and by their nonprofit nature would be less expensive than profit-maximizing private insurance companies: The CEO of one of the largest U.S. health care companies earns over $33 million a year.[15]

The company, the primary unit of economic activity, is not a fixed entity; it can be, and is being, transformed. The distinction between for-profit companies and not-for-profit charities is blurring as companies incorporate social and environmental responsibilities into their business model, not as add-ons but as intrinsic to the way that they work. Chris Meyer of the *Harvard Business Review* has called this "internalizing the externalities" of the traditional economic model of the firm. While it is easy to be cynical about this development, and it is right to criticize the "greenwashing" of otherwise unchanged corporate practice, there is also here unarguably an opportunity. Encouraged by an NGO, scores of companies are choosing to eschew high-carbon fuel sources, like oil sands.[16]

In another initiative, thousands of the world's largest companies are voluntarily publishing data on their electricity consumption and carbon emissions in a collective effort to reduce emissions, organized by another small NGO, the Carbon Disclosure Project.[17] Utilizing the power of peer and investor pressure rather than government regulation, the project organizes letters to companies representing investors holding $55 trillion, pressing them to participate and thus be scrutinized on their environmental records. Other banks are ceasing to lend to the mining companies that blast the tops off Appalachian mountains in Virginia, not because this activity is illegal—it is not— but because of the growing damage to their reputations.[18]

Consumers through their own choices can reinforce these trends: "When you're buying, you're voting," as the founder of Stonyfield Farms, the organic dairy producer, once exhorted. Every choice carries economic, political and environmental effects. It will soon be easy to monitor the labor and environmental records of manufacturers on the Web, and perhaps at the point of purchase. At projectlabel.org and other sites, the embryonic form of such indices is already visible.[19] The space is available to rethink what companies do, to realize at last that their impacts are inherently political, but also to embrace and exploit that reality. Whether this transformation is positive or negative will be determined by simple, small, everyday choices: the actions of those who compose these new commercial, social and in fact highly political entities.

A FRENCH PHILOSOPHER was once asked about the significance of May 1968, the demonstrations and eruption of spontaneous public anger in France and elsewhere.[20] He replied that the importance of May '68 was that it was the opposite of what the Communists had said was the correct manner of the revolution. The Communists had said that the revolution should be:

> Not here but somewhere else, like Cuba, Vietnam or elsewhere.
> Not now but tomorrow, in the future.
> And not you but the Communists instead, the appointed cadres.

Rejecting this injunction, the May '68ers had declared instead, "Here, Now, Us!"

THE NEXT CHAPTER SUGGESTS some core principles that might guide an individual or group wanting to take up the flag on any issue. This is a politics that offers the possibility of yet unimagined outcomes, not those defined by our current structures and ways of doing business.

This manifesto is rather short and simple. It does not proclaim a particular end-state or utopia, but instead a series of methods for *how* the individual might engage upon the issues that most concern them. The methods themselves are the message: a way of doing things that promises greater mutual concern, meaning and community of purpose.

The ends are indeed the means.

8

KILL THE KING!
NINE PRINCIPLES TO GUIDE ACTION

So much for all the theory, stories and ideas . . . what is to be done? Here is a short list of principles that may guide action, along with a few practical examples. The principles are by no means exclusive or comprehensive: mere pointers, not instructions.

1. Locate your convictions.

This is perhaps the hardest step, and I have the least useful to say about it (apart from Gandhi's and Claudette Colvin's examples, cited earlier). This must be an individual discovery of what you care most about. And this is the most fundamental point: Do not let others tell you what to care about. This can be only a *leaderless* revolution, if it is to succeed. Make up your own mind. Examine your own reactions. This is difficult in the banality yet ubiquity of contemporary culture, with its cacophony of voices and opinion. Space for contemplation is all too rare. But here's one suggestion which is doubtless revealing of my own dyspeptic disposition: What makes you angry? What never fails to irritate you for its stupidity and injustice? That may be the thing you should take up arms against. It was for me, and anger puts fuel in the tank.

2. Who's got the money, who's got the gun?

Before taking action, assess the landscape. This simple axiom will point to the main sources of influence, and obstacles. Thanks to the Internet, it is now possible to discover pretty rapidly who has a stake in any given situation, and thus who might alter it. When revolt against the dictatorial rule of Colonel Muammar Gadhafi broke out in Libya in February 2011, information on which companies were doing business with his regime was available in detail, triggering immediate pressure for these companies and individuals to disengage. The same week that the revolt broke out, several major oil companies announced their refusal to do business with the regime, under pressure from their own investors organized by a campaign group, the Genocide Intervention Network. The Sunlight Foundation published a chart of the lobbyists, including former congressmen, who were paid by Gadhafi to promote his interests. The director of the London School of Economics was forced to resign just days after the revolt began when it was revealed that his university had received substantial funds from the regime to train its elites. One welcome consequence of the vast mesh of connections that the globalized world now comprises is that even distant situations may be affected by actors close to home, who may be susceptible to pressure. Find them, use it.

3. Act as if the means are the end.

In the summer of 1968, Soviet tanks entered Czechoslovakia, crushing the "Prague spring" of growing political freedom. Massively outgunned by the Soviet tank columns, the Czechoslovak army gave way. Demonstrators attacked the tanks in city squares with stones and petrol bombs. The Soviet troops responded with machine-gun fire. One protesting student set himself on fire in Prague's Wenceslas Square. Thousands were arrested, many to be imprisoned for long sentences. The leader who had encouraged the liberalization, Alexander Dubček, was forced to capitulate, under duress signing an agreement with Moscow to reverse the reforms. Czechoslovakia endured more than another twenty years of Communism before democracy at last dawned.

That summer of '68, thousands of Czechoslovak students had traveled abroad to work. The invasion left them stranded. Among them was P., who spent the summer picking fruit in Kent. The Soviet invasion gave him a terrible choice: Should he stay in Britain, or return to Communist dictatorship? Compounding his dilemma, he had nowhere to stay. A story in *The Times* reported on the predicament of the stranded students: An organization was quickly set up to find them shelter.

My parents read the story and decided to offer refuge to the Czechoslovak student, P., who arrived shortly afterward. Though my parents that summer were caring for three children under four (my brother and I are twins, my sister twenty-three months older), and had more than enough on their plate, they gave P. a bed. He stayed for several weeks while considering what to do. After much agonizing, he eventually decided to stay in England. By chance, he had hitched a lift from a professor at Warwick University. That professor liked P. and offered him a place on his course. P.'s studies were duly arranged and he completed his degree, frequently spending his holidays at our house in South London. He went on to become an expert in fish storage. The father of two children, he now lives in Scotland.

Thirty years later my parents gave refuge once more, this time to a Zimbabwean escaping the repressive rule of Robert Mugabe. Now they were living in a smaller flat, their children long having flown the nest. My father recalled that it wasn't as simple as giving P. a room back in 1968. Asylum laws in Britain are now strictly enforced. My father was required regularly to report to the local police station that Ngoni was indeed staying with them and had not absconded. Finding study opportunities and work was also harder, though not impossible. (Universities and other such educational institutions are today themselves required to check the legal status of their foreign students, and report any noncompliance, thus, in effect, making them arms of the state.)

I asked my parents why they had taken P. in. Neither could really remember, answering my question with vague responses like "We could" or "It felt like a good thing to do." Now with my own small children, and exhausted by the tasks of their care, I marvel at my parents' hospitality.

Life is about means, not ends. There is no utopia to be gained, there is no end-state that is static and eternal, once accomplished. This was one of the great lies of Communism. Likewise, capitalism offers the great deception that thanks to its machinations everyone will be richer in the future, thus justifying gross inequality and humiliation today.

Instead it's all here, and it's all now. Nirvana tomorrow does not justify avoidable suffering now. We and our world are in constant motion, responding to each other without cease. This is one reason why Francis Fukuyama was wrong to declare "The End of History" with the triumph of liberal democracies after the collapse of Communism. No fixed state of affairs lasts forever.

4. Refer to the Cosmopolitan Criterion.

This is a pretentious way of saying give consideration to the needs of others, but based upon what *they* say are their needs, not what *we* think their needs are. The so-called Golden Rule states that you should do to others as you would be done to. This rule is often lazily touted as a universal rule applicable in all circumstances. This rule is in fact dramatically wrong, for it assumes that *we* know what *they* want or need. This logic, taken to its extreme, leads to the arrogant violence of the neoconservatives, who believe that they have the right to use force in the interests of those they are attacking, to kill people for their own good. The invasion of Iraq was clearly motivated by this logic: that the Iraqi people needed democracy, even at the cost of their own lives (we know of course that the reason was not to combat an imminent threat).[1] A hundred thousand people and perhaps more died as a result. Instability was triggered that endures, with accompanying violence, to this day. Needless to say, those advocating the war never consulted those who would do the dying for their lofty goals, whether allied soldiers or Iraq's civilians.

There is instead a much simpler way to decide what to do and how to calibrate your own action. *Ask people what they want.* They are usually more than willing to tell you.

With the Internet, ubiquitous mobile phones and Facebook, it is no longer credible to claim that we cannot find out what people "over there" are thinking. During the Arab revolutions of early 2011, pro-democracy protesters broadcast their tweets direct from Cairo's Tahrir Square, their compelling 140-character messages shattering generations-old Western stereotypes of the Middle East and the "Arab street." Websites like Global Voices now aggregate citizen reports from all over the world, but from close to the ground. And those voices are clear and fresh and urgent.

5. Address those suffering the most.

A few years ago, my wife and I traveled to northern Mali, to the southern reaches of the Sahara desert north of Timbuktu. We were on our honeymoon. We decided to take a camel tour with some Tuareg tribesmen; the trip appealed to our sense of adventure. The camels carried us far from Timbuktu into a romantic landscape of trackless desert wastes.

As night fell, we were brought to a Tuareg encampment. It turned out to be the tented home of our guide, a young Tuareg man who wore loose robes and a turban of deep blue cotton, wound around his head and neck to protect him from the blasting rays of the sun. We slept under a vast and magnificent canopy of stars, our baggage stacked around us as a barricade against the camels, who had been known to tread upon sleeping humans.

We awoke to a clear and silent dawn, and wandered to the tents to join our guide and his family for breakfast. And here the romance began to shatter. The guide's young wife sat with her baby under a rough screen. The previous evening, in the dark, their shelter had appeared as a robust canvas tent. But it turned out to be a patchwork of plastic and burlap sacks. The young woman and her baby were besieged incessantly by large swarms of flies, which would land in waves upon her and her sleeping baby's face. The woman, clearly exhausted—perhaps by hunger or illness, we could not tell—listlessly swatted the flies away, but they would settle nonetheless on the baby's eyes and lips, in swarms so thick they appeared like a blanket on the poor child's face.

Shocked, my wife and I drank our tea and ate our bread in silence. The guide's father joined us. Talking to his son, he would with horrible frequency emit an awful hacking cough. As he coughed, he doubled over in pain, his throat broadcasting the most disgusting sounds of collecting phlegm and blood, which he would periodically spit onto the sand by the fire. He clearly had tuberculosis or some other serious respiratory disease. He was desperately thin, and appeared enfeebled to the point of death.

Conversing in broken French with the guide, we asked what was wrong. The young man answered that he didn't know. The old man had never seen a doctor. But, the guide said, he had some drugs. He spoke to the old man, who pulled out a half-used packet of paracetamol, its use-by date long past. Perhaps, ventured the young man, we could give any drugs we might have. Of course we obliged, and ended up handing over perhaps a couple hundred dollars to the guide, in excessive payment for the trip. The old man had noticed my spectacles and exclaimed in delight when I handed them to him to try. I gave him these too (I had a spare pair).

We were appalled and upset by this encounter with desperate poverty. We were glad to return from the camel trip. After leaving Mali (to be honest, with some relief), however, we have not had any further contact with the guide or his family. We give some money to charity on a regular basis, but it is not in truth very much, and certainly not enough to occasion us any significant limits on our own consumption.

How should one respond to suffering? Consider two contrasting answers to this question. In a recent book, the philosopher Peter Singer uses an example to illustrate our obligation to others, including those far away who may be unknown to us.[2] A small girl is drowning in a lake in front of you and you are the only person who can rescue the child. You are, however, wearing expensive shoes, which will be ruined if you dive in to rescue the girl. Singer believes, of course, that the answer to such a dilemma is clear and accepted by almost everyone: You must dive in to save the child, but ruin the shoes.

Singer argues that in reality the crisis of the drowning child is presented to us constantly. Every minute, at least eighteen children die of hunger and preventable disease: twenty-seven thousand every day. It costs, moreover, far less than the price of your shoes to save them. Just as if the child were drowning directly in front of us, the moral imperative is clear and precise: We must act, even if there is a cost to ourselves, albeit a small one. Using calculations by economist Jeffrey Sachs and others, Singer suggests that if all people in the rich world gave a mere 1 percent of their income, poverty and preventable disease in the world could be effectively eradicated. Singer has set up a website where individuals can make such pledges.* He reportedly donates 25 percent of his own income to charity.

At the other end of the moral spectrum, nineteenth-century German über-anarchist Max Stirner believed that the idea of morality is basically absurd and manufactured by those who cloak their selfish purposes in pseudo-universal principles which have no other origin. There is no such thing as society (as Margaret Thatcher too once famously observed). It is instead individuals and their own desires which matter. Thus, individuals are required to do nothing but follow their own wishes to the fullest, wherever this may lead. To do

---

*www.thelifeyoucansave.com.

anything else is to act falsely and to invite falseness from others in response, thus risking an order—or rather, disorder—based on dishonest and manufactured ideas.

Stirner's ideas imply that we have no obligation to dive in to save the child in Singer's thought experiment. Almost everyone would find this appalling. Yet, as Singer has observed, this is what we consistently do. Very few individuals give even 1 percent of their income to those worse off than they. Several thousand people have made such pledges at Singer's website, but of course this is but a tiny drop in the bucket. Most rich governments have failed to fulfill their own oft-repeated pledges to commit 0.7 percent of their GDP to development aid. The funds required to meet the UN's Millennium Development Goals, established in 2000 as achievable targets to reduce poverty and disease, have not been provided, including by the G8, G20 and UN General Assembly, which have on repeated occasions, promised all efforts to do so.

So what's the flaw with Singer's reasoning? Why are we unconvinced to help the distant poor? Are we inherently selfish, more Max Stirner than Peter Singer? It is easy for a moralist to say that the needs of a Somali woman dying in childbirth should be as compelling to us as if she were our sister. But, as Singer has disappointingly discovered, such reasoning has little lasting impact.

If a child drowns before us, how tiny would be the minority who refused to act because they didn't want to get their expensive shoes wet, and what would the majority do to that person once they found out? Somehow we need to find a way to stimulate the emotional connection that evokes compassion, an emotion that, unlike moral rules, seems shared among humanity (with some sociopathic exceptions). How is compassion between people generated? One clear and straightforward answer presents itself: the encounter.

Missing in the reasoning of Singer is any sense of what Stirner, by contrast, believed necessary, intrinsic and inevitable—engagement. Stirner firmly rejected any a priori assumption of what such engagement might produce, least of all that it should result in an obligation to render help to others. But it makes sense that engagement produces a different kind of reaction, and a different conversation, than mere knowledge. It is clearly not enough to know that people "out there" are suffering. But locate oneself next to that suffering, as my wife and I found in the Malian desert, and the reaction becomes entirely different, even though the facts and our knowledge of them remain exactly the same.

Thus nineteenth-century Stirner may paradoxically provide a truer guide to action in the connected twenty-first century than contemporary philosophers who, with great humanity, urge that we accept the obligation to rescue the drowning child. For it is engagement—or rather, its absence—that may precisely explain why the Singers, and the proponents of the UN Millennium Development Goals, or the 0.7 percent goal, or the Bonos or Angelinas have failed to convince those who have so much to hand over even a little bit, and make a huge life-saving difference, to the billions who have so desperately little.

And from this, one conclusion stands out: States, borders and indeed institutions in general must by their very nature limit our engagement with one another; they channel, frame, render detached and sometimes obstruct the vast mêlée of human interaction. And by limiting that engagement, somewhere along the way our compassion is eviscerated. The requirement for engagement, as demanded too by the Cosmopolitan Criterion (above), is reinforced.

The twenty-first century offers engagement at levels unprecedented in human history. As Kwame Anthony Appiah observes in his elegant study *Cosmopolitanism: Ethics in a World of Strangers*, a stroller along New York's Fifth Avenue will pass more nationalities in half an hour than an ancient Roman would have met in a lifetime. The multihued society of America, Britain, Europe and more or less everywhere, increasingly, offers commensurately varied chances for encounters with the hitherto distant Other, be they Somali, Kyrgyz, Malay or Tongan. "Abroad" is more and more located right here. At least four hundred million people now live in countries not of their birth. And these are just the first-generation immigrants; add a second and third generation, and the proportion grows much higher. Over two million of London's more than seven and a half million inhabitants were born overseas. Heterogeneity will become routine. Whether we like it or not, we will have to engage.

The sharp and unprecedented increases in immigration in almost all developed countries, driving commensurate increases in ethnic diversity, have triggered anguished debates in Europe and the U.S. In Switzerland, a popular referendum affirmed a ban on mosque construction, though there are very few mosques already. In the Netherlands, the 2010 general election saw a significant swing to the far-right anti-immigration party of Geert Wilders. In the U.S., Arizona enacted a law allowing police to stop anyone merely on suspicion of being an illegal immigrant.

And at first sight, it appears that fears of the effect of an influx of outsiders on established stable societies are well placed. Harvard sociologist Robert Putnam has found that the more mixed a society, the lower its indices of "social capital"—trust, altruism, associations, active cooperation—and the higher its indices of social fragmentation—crime, for instance.[3] But crucially, he found that these reductions in social solidarity and "social capital" were *short-term* effects. At first, it appears, local societies "hunker down"; trust declines, even within members of the same race or ethnic group. People retreat into privacy.

In the longer run, however, the outcomes are more positive. New forms of association and social solidarity emerge. In more hybrid societies, there is more creativity—as measured, for instance, by the number of Nobel Prizes. Immigration is associated with more rapid economic growth, although short-term effects should not be overlooked, particularly on the lowest paid who tend to feel first the effects of more intensified competition for jobs from immigrants.

The evidence suggests that immigration from the global south to the global north greatly enhances development in the south, partly because of the flow of remittances from new immigrants to their families "back home," but also because of the transfer of technology and new ideas through immigrant networks. This effect is reportedly so powerful that it may offset the "brain drain" costs to the southern countries sending the migrants. Putnam cites evidence of yet greater positive effect, including a World Bank study that estimates that increasing annual northward immigration by only 3 percentage points might produce net benefits greater than meeting all national (U.S.) targets for development assistance *plus* canceling all Third World debt *plus* abolishing all barriers to Third World trade.

A further reason to address those suffering the most is simply this: Here, you can make the most difference.

6. Consult and negotiate.

When I was responsible for sanctions policy on Iraq at the UK Mission to the United Nations, we were often approached by campaigning NGOs who wanted us to alter our policies, and lift or amend sanctions in order to end the humanitarian suffering in Iraq. They were right, of course, but that didn't mean that they were effective.

In general, I avoided meeting these campaigners, well aware that I would be subjected to a rhetorical finger-wagging session. It was difficult for campaigners to find out who was dealing with Iraq in our mission, and we didn't make it easy for them (it's still very difficult, even though now the mission has the inevitable official website, as opaque as the smoked glass at the mission's entrance). Only rarely did the campaigners manage to identify me, and persuade me to meet them.

Such meetings were tedious and predictable. Invariably, the campaigners would march into my office, then lecture me about the immorality of what my government was doing, demanding change— but rarely specifying in any detail what that change should be: just change! Discussion would be tense and confrontational; the meetings would end with much relief, for me at least. I sensed too that the objective for the campaigners was often the fact of the meeting, which they could now parade as effective action on their part, the meeting alone amounting to a victory. Of course, it was not.

No doubt such lobbying made them feel better. But the effect on me was to make me more determined to avoid such future encounters. Thanks to the superficiality of the campaigners' arguments, I was able easily to dismiss them. They forgot that I worked on Iraq full-time every day, and was steeped in the arguments and data to justify and defend our policies.

Two academics from Notre Dame University in Indiana used a different approach. They approached the individual officials involved in the British and U.S. governments, asking to collect information about our policies. They were polite and patient. They came to meet me several times. After several meetings, they offered a detailed set of proposals to change our policy, ideas that addressed our concerns to limit Iraq's potential to rearm while minimizing the potential negative humanitarian effects of sanctions. The U.S. State Department held a discussion with many officials who wanted to meet the academics and hear their proposals. Eventually, their ideas were adopted as British–American policy and led to a major amendment of sanctions policy, which was put into place in 2002.*

It was too late, and such a policy should have been enacted from the beginning of comprehensive sanctions on Iraq in 1990. But the point is clear.

Negotiation should ideally be direct, not through intermediaries. When my wife and I bought our apartment in New York City, we were represented in the negotiations by our real estate agent and eventually by a lawyer. The negotiations quickly deteriorated. Every move by the seller was scrutinized for deviousness, every motive and communication was immediately placed under suspicion. When the seller sought to delay the sale after we had agreed on a price, this was seized upon as a sign of "bad faith." Lawyers reported antagonistic exchanges. As stalemate beckoned, we proposed a meeting with the sellers. Tense and anticipating a conflict, we arrived at the apartment, to find—needless to say—a perfectly affable couple who merely wanted to stay in the apartment for a few weeks before their new home was ready. For them the alternative was to take their small children to live in a hotel.

No the point is by the time those with conscience get up to speed, it is always too late. The point is the gov. should not be asking before policy is implemented.

---

*The new sanctions policy altered controls on exports to Iraq so that everything was permitted except goods that appeared on a "control list" of items that might be used for weapons manufacture. Previously, nothing could be exported to Iraq except goods that were expressly permitted, case-by-case, by the UN sanctions committee (with some exceptions).

7. "Big picture, small deeds."

The innovation company ?What If! offers this maxim as a way to overcome the inertia that too often stymies change. ?What If! trains employees in how to be innovative; it found that sometimes, though inspired by their training away-day, trainees would still fail to implement the techniques they had learned. It was simply too overwhelming to change the prevailing culture of their everyday workplace. To counter this problem, ?What If! proposed a simple philosophy: Keep in mind the overall change you wish to achieve, but act a little every day to make it reality.

Though transposed to the corporate world, this technique echoes the "small steps" proposed by Mahatma Gandhi to achieve profound and enduring change. There is an ancient Chinese proverb to the same effect (the Internet tells me): "It is better to take many small steps in the right direction than to make a great leap forward only to stumble backward," sage advice that Mao Zedong clearly ignored in forcing China's Great Leap Forward in the 1960s, which forced peasants from their land and led to the starvation and death of perhaps more than thirty million. Possibly recognizing this catastrophe, Mao's successor Deng Xiaoping proposed a more pragmatic method of change: "crossing the river by feeling the stones."

This metaphor is both more compelling and offers a more pragmatic approach: Stones are palpable, material, solid. The steps of any strategy should be concrete; not rhetorical but practical. Internet campaigns clearly fail this criterion; volunteering at a local school does not. Mahatma Gandhi distilled the epic struggle against British colonial rule into a simple but practical act that anyone could undertake: making salt.

And the goal must be epic. The spirit soars at the momentous

Small steps are always "too late"

challenge, not the banal. Break that challenge down into small, practical, daily tasks, and get to work. Though the steps toward it may be
humble, find a goal that is great: End poverty, prevent war, save the
planet. Locate your objective, grasp your flag, then march deliberately toward the enemy. If you do so with courage and conviction,
others will surely follow.

as if you don't have to work and can spend your whole time doing. What gov. workers do while getting a good salary + paid time off.

8. Use nonviolence.
Alexander Berkman was an anarchist who passionately detested the
widespread exploitation and abuse of workers in industrial America
of the late nineteenth century. An immigrant from Russia, he was
influenced by anarchist thinkers and groups in New York City, where
he became a close friend of the famous anarchist Emma Goldman.
As told by Goldman in her autobiography, *My Life*, and Berkman in
his *Prison Memoirs of an Anarchist*, both were deeply affected by the
Haymarket affair—or massacre, as it is sometimes known: the name
of the event an indicator, as it often is, of the prejudices of the namer.

On May 4, 1886, at Haymarket Square in Chicago, at a rally in
support of striking workers, an unknown person threw a bomb at
police as they dispersed the gathering. The bomb blast and ensuing
gunfire resulted in the deaths of eight police officers and an unknown
number of civilians. In the trial that followed, eight anarchists were
tried for murder despite paltry evidence against them. Four were put
to death, and one committed suicide in prison. The judge declared,
"Not because you have caused the Haymarket bomb, but because
you are Anarchists, you are on trial." To this day, debate continues
about the true identity of the bomber.

It is clear from both Goldman's and Berkman's memoirs that they were radicalized by what they saw as a profound injustice. Both came to believe that only dramatic and, if necessary, violent acts—the *attentat*—would galvanize the working population to rise up against a deeply unjust system. The opportunity for such an act was soon to present itself.

In June 1892, workers at a steel plant in Homestead, Pennsylvania, were locked out after pay negotiations failed between the Carnegie Steel Company and the Amalgamated Association of Iron and Steel Workers. The result was one of the first organized strikes in American labor history. Andrew Carnegie had placed his factories, and indeed later his industrial empire, under the control of Henry Clay Frick. Carnegie publicly supported the rights of workers to join unions and employ collective bargaining. Privately, however, he encouraged Frick to break the strike and, with it, the union.

Frick locked the union workers out and placed barbed-wire fences, searchlights and watchtowers around the factory. He hired nonunion workers to take the strikers' jobs and get the factory going again, but they were unable to break through the union's picket lines. So Frick hired three hundred armed guards from the Pinkerton Detective Agency to break the picket lines. When the Pinkerton guards arrived at the factory on the morning of July 6, a gunfight broke out. Nine union workers and seven guards were killed during the fight, which lasted twelve hours.

There was widespread outrage at Frick's actions and the violent attack of the "Pinkertons." Berkman and Goldman decided to assassinate Frick. This was the opportunity for the violent *attentat* to rouse the working class to revolt. There was no viler capitalist than Frick: For a while, he was known as "America's most hated man." In his memoir, Berkman recounts his romantic fascination with the extreme act:

Could anything be nobler than to die for a grand, a sublime Cause? Why, the very life of a true revolutionist has no other purpose, no significance whatever, save to sacrifice it on the altar of the beloved People.

Berkman's execution of the plan, however, was amateurish. His plan was to assassinate Frick and commit suicide afterward; Goldman's role was to explain Berkman's motives after his death. First, Berkman tried to make a bomb, but he failed. Berkman and Goldman then pooled their meager savings to buy a handgun and a suit for Berkman to wear for the assassination attempt.

On July 23, 1892, Berkman entered Frick's office armed with a gun and a sharpened steel file. Frick dived under a chair and began to yell. Berkman shot Frick three times, then grappled with him and stabbed him in the leg. Others in the office came to Frick's rescue and beat Berkman unconscious. He was convicted of attempted murder and given a twenty-two-year prison sentence. Frick survived the attack.

As he later related in his memoir, Berkman encountered a Homestead striker soon after his imprisonment. Berkman immediately romanticizes the man as the embodiment of the workers' struggle. He is enthralled to meet an actual striker, a true-blooded member of the working classes. Here at last Berkman would find his vindication. But the meeting produces nothing but bitter disappointment. The striker decries Berkman's assassination attempt. "We are law-abiding people," he says, adding that the workers don't want anything to do with the "anachrists," as he misnames them.

Other workers on whose behalf Berkman made the *attentat* were not impressed either. There was no worker uprising as a result of Berkman's effort; his attack was widely condemned, by, among others, unions, workers and even other anarchists. Negative publicity from the attempted assassination resulted in the collapse of the Homestead strike. Twenty-five hundred men lost their jobs, and most of the workers who stayed had their wages halved.

If not violence, then what? All too often, the debate is framed as violence or nothing; pacifism as mere inactivity. As the world contemplated how to respond to Colonel Gadhafi's brutal repression of unrest in Libya, media commentators dwelt on the debate over the imposition of no-fly zones or other forms of military intervention, ignoring the many various nonmilitary but nonetheless coercive measures available: These were complicated, and thus ill-suited to the Punch and Judy requirements of sound-bite debate.[4] The whole framing of such debates suggests that violence is strong, the absence of violence weak. Pacifism is invariably portrayed as a kind of "do nothing" philosophy.

Nonviolence resolves this problem. Nonviolent methods are not doing nothing. Instead, they are forceful methods that can be highly effective but avoid injury and bloodshed, while gaining moral authority from the rejection of violence.

To get down to specifics, nonviolent action can take many different forms. In his essential and concise essay "From Dictatorship to Democracy," Gene Sharp lists no fewer than 198 different nonviolent methods, but here are three.*

Boycott: The word "boycott" entered the English language thanks to Captain Charles Boycott, the land agent of an absentee landlord in Ireland. In 1880, harvests had been poor, so the landlord offered his tenants a 10 percent reduction in their rents. The tenants de-

---

*I also recommend Mark Kurlansky's *Nonviolence: The History of a Dangerous Idea* (New York: Modern Library, 2009).

manded a 25 percent reduction, but were refused. Boycott then attempted to evict eleven tenants from the land. The Irish nationalist Charles Stewart Parnell proposed that ostracism was more powerful than violence: Greedy landlords and land agents like Boycott should be made pariahs. Despite the short-term economic hardship they incurred, Boycott's workers stopped work in the fields and stables, as well as in his house. Local businessmen stopped trading with him, and the postman refused to deliver mail. Boycott soon found himself isolated and unable to hire anyone to harvest the crops. Eventually, fifty outsiders volunteered to do the work, but they had to be escorted by a thousand policemen and soldiers, even though local leaders had said there would be no violence, and none materialized. This protection ended up costing far more than the harvest was worth. After the harvest, the "boycott" was successfully continued.

Gandhi organized a boycott of British goods. In Montgomery, Alabama, African-Americans boycotted segregated buses. The National Negro Convention boycotted slave-produced goods in 1830. Today boycotts are even easier to organize, thanks to the Internet. The Dutch bank ING was forced to cancel bonuses for its senior staff after thousands of customers threatened to withdraw their deposits, and thus risk a run on the bank. A Facebook and Twitter boycott campaign erupted after news emerged that the chief executive was to be awarded a €1.25 million bonus despite the fact the bank had received €10 billion in state aid to keep afloat, and had frozen pensions and given staff only a 1 percent pay raise. Dutch politicians later voted for a 100 percent retrospective tax on all bonuses paid to executives at institutions that had received state aid as a result of the financial crisis.[5]

Isolate: The withdrawal of social approval for individuals is distressing to those subjected to it. Public shaming is an underutilized tool. To politicians and public figures who bask in public attention, its denial can be painful indeed.

In New York City, a number of women were fed up with the harassment they routinely faced in public, on subways and the street, ranging from unwelcome sexual comments to groping and stalking. Frustrated with cultural attitudes that suggested such abuse was an inevitable price of being a woman, they formed a group to fight back. Emily May founded Hollaback! (www.ihollaback.org) with friends in 2005. Today it has chapters in six American cities, along with others in Britain, Canada and Australia. The group has recently developed an iPhone application to allow women immediately to log and report such incidents and, if possible, photograph the perpetrators. The aim is to produce a comprehensive picture and identify hotspots of such harassment, citywide and even nationwide. Reports will be forwarded to police for action, including particular zones of repeated activity. But there are obvious obstacles for the police to press convictions—they cannot solve the problem alone. By identifying and exhibiting the photographs of perpetrators, the group also hopes to shame the men who carry out the abuse, and create new cultural attitudes to replace the old: to render harassment socially unacceptable.[6]

In a more international context, a white farmer in newly independent Zimbabwe once told me that the economic and political isolation of white minority-dominated Rhodesia may not have undermined the economy sufficiently to force the Rhodesian government to give up its apartheid practices. We could survive economically, she told me, but once we were under international sanctions, she said, we knew one thing with certainty—that white minority rule could not last forever.

Sabotage: This method is to be used only in the most extreme circumstances of gross injustice and repression, when other nonviolent methods have failed. A recent illustration of the inherent risks and ambiguous consequences of sabotage, even of the nonviolent kind, is the story of the Stuxnet computer worm, which appears to have been deliberately designed to interfere with Iran's nuclear program. The worm was highly sophisticated, suggesting that states (perhaps the United States) were behind its creation. Concealing itself in the operating system of computers that control industrial mechanisms, Stuxnet reportedly works by speeding up the gas centrifuges used to enrich uranium so that the centrifuges are damaged or destroyed. All the while, the control systems continue to indicate that everything is normal. The effects of Stuxnet are not clear, and Iran has admitted to only limited damage from the virus. Illustrating the dangers of using such techniques, however, there is now debate that the way has been cleared for others to use similar devices—which are effectively sabotage, albeit by the most modern methods. In effect, a new front has been opened in conflict, with few rules to govern it. As one journalist put it: "We have crossed a threshold and there is no turning back."[7] There are now belated calls for new international agreements to prohibit such cyberwarfare, while others comment that enforcement of such rules would in any case be all but impossible, given the intrinsic anonymity and complexity of the Web. If you are going to use these tools, it would be wise to be sure that they cannot then be turned against you. Hence the requirement to use nonviolent sabotage only in extremis.

But for all the drawbacks of sabotage, it has one signal and perhaps overriding virtue: It doesn't kill people.

In Wim Wenders's film *Wings of Desire,* an old man is in a library contemplating images of dead children. He is very elderly and perhaps dying. He thinks to himself, "My heroes are no longer the warriors and kings, but the things of peace. . . . But so far no one has succeeded in singing an epic of peace. What is it about peace that its inspiration is not enduring? Why is its story so hard to tell?"

9. Kill the King!

Chess may be useless as a metaphor for international relations but it carries one very important lesson. The only point of the game is to take the opponent's king. All other moves, and elegant plays with bishop or pawns, are but preliminary to this object. Do not be satisfied with process, but only with results. A campaign to end genocide, richly adorned with expensive video and glamorous celebrities, is worth nothing if it doesn't save a single life. Don't campaign for others to perform the action required to achieve change: Do it yourself. Sending a text message or signing an Internet petition is likely to achieve nothing, given that so little went into it.

The measure of any political action is not how many hits you get on the campaign website, how many followers you may have on Twitter, or supporters on your Facebook page. The measure is effects in the real world on the thing you are trying to change: Are there fewer nuclear weapons? Has the dictator been overthrown? Is one child saved from starvation?

Alexander the Great always aimed his forces at his enemy's strongest point. When that fell, the enemy collapsed. Kill the King!

INDIVIDUALLY, these principles are unexceptionable. Who can object to nonviolent, step-by-step action, negotiated with those affected, and designed to address those most suffering? But taken together, these principles in fact amount to a radically different form of political action from the contemporary cultural model, which seems by contrast to amount to very little: Vote for the government, maybe campaign a little to ask others to do things you want, and, if you're directly concerned, perhaps lobby government. The principles suggested above offer a rather more vigorous, directed but above all effective, even transformative, course of action. This is perhaps why there is such establishment hostility to these methods, and indeed to the word "anarchism," including the very peaceful and collaborative form proposed here: The employment of these methods will actually change things, including by changing the way that things change. Those who benefit from the current status quo don't want you to know that.

One person following these principles will not cause a global revolution, though he may revolutionize his own life. But the action of one may stimulate others. And if many adopt these principles, a revolution, a leaderless revolution, will eventually become manifest.

9

CONCLUSION:
A VISION OF THE HUMAN

In Tolstoy's *War and Peace*, some of the greatest scenes are those depicting the battles of the Franco-Russian wars. Cannonballs from Napoleon's artillery whizz overhead, cavalry horses rear and flare at fusillades of musket fire, men quiver with fear and red flows their blood.

In one scene during the Battle of Austerlitz, the Russian troops are taken by surprise by advancing French columns that suddenly emerge from the engulfing fog. As the French fire scatters them, the Russian front collapses and men flee in disarray. Weeping with anger and shame as he contemplates imminent defeat, Prince Andrew picks up a standard that a retreating officer has let fall. Heedless of the danger and the bullets cracking all around him, he gives a cry "piercing as a child's" and runs forward.[1]

His singular action is enough to rally the disordered infantrymen around him. Suddenly, one soldier moves, and then another, and soon the whole battalion runs forward shouting "Hurrah!" and overtakes him. Surrounded by charging troops, Prince Andrew runs forward, now just twenty paces from the French guns, so close that he sees the fear and anger on the gunners' faces. Prince Andrew is struck down; others seize the flag to maintain the advance.

The battle is, however, lost. Later, Prince Andrew, now captured, lies gravely wounded in a French dressing station. Napoleon visits the injured Russians. Close to death, Prince Andrew is unmoved by the sight of his erstwhile hero. Looking into Napoleon's eyes, "Prince Andrew thought of the insignificance of greatness, the unimportance of life which no one could understand, and the still greater unimportance of death, the meaning of which no one alive could understand or explain." Tolstoy's battle scenes are of the microcosmic actions upon which pivots victory or defeat. These actions are not the function of the decisions of generals or emperors; they are the contingent decisions of individual officers and soldiers, like the courageous if ultimately futile charge of Prince Andrew. In an earlier chapter, the Battle of Schöngrabern is turned by the decision of one man, Timókhin, to charge the French lines, armed only with a sword. Such actions, almost random in appearance, are for Tolstoy what matters, not grand strategy or great men.

In his seminal essay "The Hedgehog and the Fox," Isaiah Berlin analyzed Tolstoy's view of history. *War and Peace*, according to Berlin, illustrates Tolstoy's skepticism of an account that suggested that events were under the control of leaders, states or governments. Such history, Tolstoy believed, accounted for not more than 0.001 percent of human affairs; it was, moreover, basically false. At Austerlitz, the Russian czar and his generals are described standing on a hilltop observing their troops descend into the thick fog enveloping the valley beneath them. It is a figurative illustration of their true knowledge, Tolstoy suggests. The chief Russian general, Kutúzov, enjoys heroic stature in Russian history, but Tolstoy portrays him groaning helplessly as his troops are attacked by surprise. Only Prince Andrew is decisive in response to the emerging catastrophe, and his response is not to issue orders but to seize the fallen flag and advance.

In Tolstoy's descriptions, real life was far too complex and contingent to be controlled by those at the summit of the pyramid. In fact, they could not be expected to understand it at all, because they were not part of it or close enough to witness it. Those who claimed such understanding were either naive or were claiming knowledge for some other purpose—to wield power, for instance. In fact, as *War and Peace* shows, it is those at the base of the pyramid who make history, even if they do not know it.

This chimes with our own intuition. Battles are as life: the strange and inconstant mix of circumstance, random events and our own volition. Each is crucial; none is separable. The abstraction from this mix into a linear, polished narrative is inherently false. Equally false is any claim that human action is driven by a singular motive, such as the requirement to "maximize utility," as some economists would claim. Under scrutiny, any event, however great or small, is revealed as a fantastic and hugely complex mix of influence and causation, some inconsequential, some crucial. There is no base, no bottom to these causes and effects, all are contingent upon others.

Tolstoy's hostility was directed against those who pretended that history was of great men and their decisions, a depiction he believed fundamentally inaccurate and dishonest. But it is not only historians who must reduce. Governments too are required to aggregate the world's incredible complexity into simple truths, to take the billions of actions and wishes of their populations and claim that they can be aggregated. This adduces no malign purpose to governments; they have no alternative but to reduce in this way. They are required to do so in order to claim that they understand, in order that they can produce policies and decisions that offer to arbitrate the complexity.

"The Hedgehog and the Fox" is celebrated as a superb analysis of Tolstoy's writing and historical views. Oddly, however, Berlin does not explore how Tolstoy's writing, and the view of history intrinsic in it, informed the writer's politics, instead concentrating on the more mystical aspects of Tolstoy's thought. For Tolstoy believed that all authority impeded the power of independent action by individuals—and that only the individual had any authentic understanding of their circumstance and how to change it. Tolstoy was an anarchist.

Tolstoy believed that it was those at the base of the pyramid—the foot soldiers on the battlefields of Borodino or Austerlitz—who in fact made history. The "great men" and generals who claimed to understand it had not a clue. For Tolstoy, it was ironic that historians looked to the generals and leaders for the decisions that determined history, rather than the infantry. More ironic still was that the infantrymen did so too.

THE DOMINATING THOUGHT-SYSTEMS of the twentieth century hold only fragmentary clues to the remedies necessary today. Communism offered a spurious equality at the sacrifice of individual liberty. Capitalism offers liberty at the expense of social justice, harmony and that essential sense of individual or shared meaning.

Both left and right do, however, offer hints of a new and stronger philosophy. The greatest strength of the right has been its appeal to individual enterprise and self-expression, freed of the deadening burden of government. That of the left is its recognition that we are not separated from one another, that community embraces and succors all, opposing injustice, inequality and a merely selfish and ultimately divisive individualism. We are all better off together.

But the economic theory underlying capitalism and Communist orthodoxy offer a very limited and ultimately negative view of the human. In neoclassical economic theory, it is claimed without evidence that people are basically self-seeking, that they want above all the satisfaction of their material desires. The ultimate objective of mankind is economic growth, and that is maximized only through raw, and lightly regulated, competition. If the rewards of this system are spread unevenly, that is a necessary price. Others on the planet are to be regarded as either customers, competitors or factors of production. Effects upon the planet itself are mere "externalities" to the model, with no reckoning of the cost—at least for now. Nowhere in this analysis appear factors such as human cooperation, love, trust, compassion or hatred, curiosity or beauty. Nowhere appears the concept of meaning. What cannot be measured is ignored. But the trouble is that once our basic needs for shelter and food have been met, such factors may be the most important of all.

In Marxist theory, the proletariat should eventually be freed of all burdens, including of government. But in practice, all Communist systems rapidly established and maintained huge bureaucracies, with their privileged elites, to instruct the people on their best interests. Never were they to be asked what these might be. Those who offered a dissenting voice were repressed, often with great cruelty. In suppressing the anarchists of the Spanish Republic, or the Bolsheviks of the Kronstadt rebellion in 1921, the Communists showed their true colors. Communism could never mean freedom from authority. *That* revolution would never be permitted. The people were not to be trusted.

The methods discussed here instead imply a different view of mankind. That people can be trusted successfully to manage their own affairs, to negotiate with one another, to regulate their own societies from the bottom up—by moral rules, rather than coercion and punishment. That there is more available than the ugliness, conflict and emptiness of contemporary society. Cynics will argue that such trust is misplaced, and that conflict is inevitable. But the evidence from the few occasions when people have been given true agency over their affairs suggests rather the opposite: respect, consensus, or at worst an acceptance of difference. If all authority disappeared today, our current condition of mistrust and fear would guarantee the "war of all against all." But the practices offered here would, with time, build trust anew. It even may be built into something never experienced before, something extraordinary and beautiful—a new society, governed by itself.

THE PREPARATION of this book has concluded just as something extraordinary has begun. In the Middle East, mass protests have driven dictators from power in Tunisia and Egypt. In Libya, an uprising, with outside military support, has deposed the repressive Gadhafi regime. And in America and Europe, mass popular protest has broken out against the injustice of the current political and economic system. The Occupy Wall Street movement may currently count only a few thousand people, but it seems to represent a much wider disillusionment and anger with the status quo. As I write these words, the protests have spread across the United States and Western Europe.

There is a whiff of revolution in the air—and not only in the Middle East. We have perhaps arrived at one of those moments of history where fundamental change becomes possible, as people awaken to the profound injustices, but also incapability, of the current dispensation. In an echo of Thomas Kuhn's theory of paradigm shifts in scientific belief, the old paradigm of politics and economics is appearing more and more inadequate. A new paradigm cries out to emerge.

As this book has argued, protest alone is unlikely to be sufficient when the political system, although ostensibly democratic, has been co-opted by the rich and the powerful. It is implausible to expect such a system to deliver, for instance, necessary banking reform, when banking CEOs enjoy far greater access to the political system than ordinary voters. Just read the newspapers.

A new system needs to be created. What that system should consist of has been laid out in this book. At Zuccotti Park in downtown Manhattan, where the Occupy Wall Street protests have been centered, some of the attributes of a new system have been evident.

Instead of a hierarchy, decisions among the protesters are made by consensus. Everyone who wants to gets a chance to speak. Each night, a "general assembly" of the protesters is convened. There are no leaders, but it is organized. And amazingly, everyone respects the common rules. When one speaks, nobody interrupts. Though the police have banned bullhorns and microphones, across the square other people echo the words of the speaker so that every one of the hundreds present can listen. Paradoxically, this has had the effect of binding the group more closely together. Even the act of one person speaking is now, thanks to the "human mike," more involving. Astonishingly, it feels like an intimate conversation, but among hundreds of people.

But the drawbacks of this form of protest are also evident. There is no list of demands. No one claims to speak for all the protesters, so there is no single common message save, perhaps, "Enough!" This has confounded many commentators and journalists, accustomed perhaps to more directed and traditional forms of protest. What do you want? they ask. But if one would-be leader were to stand up with a manifesto, others would surely protest that no one has the right to sum up their demands. As I heard one man exclaim, with some passion, "I don't want anyone to speak for me!"

A more succinct plea for direct involvement in politics and our future could hardly be spoken.

But for such protests to amount to anything, change must be inspired that can be transmitted across the system, and not confined to a few thousand idealists on the streets. It must be change that anyone, with a will, can undertake.

WHAT MIGHT this consist of?

The economy can be changed from the inside out by altering the basic model of the company, from privately owned profit-seeking, to cooperative benefit. Cooperative companies, owned by their employees (or rather, partners), can be both competitive and fair, and more fulfilling for all involved. They can hardwire justice as part of their construction—for instance, by declaring a commitment that the highest-paid employee is paid no more than, say, five times the lowest. By making every worker a partner, they can create an entirely different culture of the workplace, where everyone has a voice—and a stake—in success, in contrast to the latent antagonism between highly paid bosses and minimally paid employees.

Then the choice is for all of us to encourage such companies with our patronage. Thus, this culture, this new way of doing things, can spread, an organic change to the nature of the economy. As cooperative companies multiply, they can form collaborative networks, where business-to-business transactions reinforce the trend, which one day may then become the norm. The genesis of such networks is already visible, in efforts like solidarityNYC.org, a website that lists the many businesses that promote values—sustainability, economic justice—other than mere profit. Already, the site covers a vast range of goods and services, from food basics to financial services. It can be done, but it involves a choice.

Other changes are possible too, though none will come about by the natural forces of the market—or by government legislation.

How might we replace the currently iniquitous and risky financial sector, where risk taking has been ensured by the taxpayer but the profits go only to the bankers—a system that not only is grossly unfair, but also has put the entire global economy in jeopardy? In Canada, the third-largest national bank is a credit union. As an illustration of the stranglehold of the profit-seeking banks on Washington, such a national bank is all but impossible in the U.S., with the obstacles in federal legislation, the result of intensive and wholly self-interested lobbying by the commercial banks.

But it is not implausible to imagine a cooperatively owned bank that is not just national, but international, and able to reap the economies of scale currently enjoyed only by the big private banks. Cynics will snigger at the idealism of such a venture, but the cynic, as Oscar Wilde once observed, knows the price of everything, but not its value. No one pretends that the challenge is easy, yet to imagine it is a start.

It is the same story with politics or, to put it more accurately, the method of deciding our future. It is hard to find anyone in America who still believes in the current political system. Indeed, even politicians must attack "politics as usual" in order to stand a chance of being elected. Yet here too, there is widespread cynicism that any improvement is possible. The problem seems just too big. We shrug and sigh with deepening despair, but nothing is done to change it.

Taking control of our affairs must start with doing just that. The necessary change will not come from above, however much we wish for it. The habit of taking a full part in decisions about the things that matter to us must start small, like the participatory decision-making at Zuccotti Park. At the schools our children attend, parents and teachers can form collective groups to debate the school's business. Whatever the rules of the school, those that run it, including the local authorities, must pay heed.

The same can be done at other local institutions, including hospitals or parks. Participation—and government of our own affairs—starts to become habitual and the norm. Local residents can come together to debate local concerns, from muggings to tree-planting. This is how self-government can begin.

AND THIS IS KEY. At no point does this book propose violent revolution, or the overthrow of the existing system, or indeed anything illegal except perhaps in resisting the most vicious repression. This is a revolution that can, and perhaps should, come about gradually, changing minds and customs day by day. It is a revolution that will come about through small actions, starting with a few, but then spreading to the many, a revolution that will come about through demonstrating the value of this new way of doing things—*show, don't tell*—and neither forcing others nor lecturing them, and least of all ramming change down unyielding throats.

Gradually then, and by force of example, self-government of the many by the many can become the norm. Networks of cooperation will emerge, reinforcing positive change elsewhere. Borders need not be an obstacle. In a highly connected world, they are arguably less and less relevant. The most effective international networks of the twenty-first century have been terrorists and criminal syndicates. They have already recognized and exploited the true nature of the world today. We must replace them with better and more powerful bonds of mutual cooperation, untrammeled by archaic boundaries.

Ultimately, such bonds offer a greater stability than the fragile if logical-seeming architecture of state-based interaction, which is in fact secured upon very uncertain foundations: the false calculus of a state's "interests." Instead, these would be deeper and broader flows of collaboration, entailing the real and enacted interests and ideals of peoples cooperating, en masse. Indeed, the failure of the state-based system in managing our most worrying problems—economic volatility, climate change—indicates that the system itself may now be the problem, for it is more perpetuating this instability than solving it.

Again, this is not to propose the abolition of the international diplomatic system, or the demolition of the United Nations. Instead, it is about a more fundamental shift in our models—and practice— of human cooperation. But it is a shift involving the *doing* of a new way, slowly replacing the old, simply by being better and rendering the earlier obsolete.

After working within government, I stopped believing that protest or campaigning can deliver real justice and enduring change, even if such methods can call attention to urgent need. The current system is far too deeply entrenched. Small but important battles for justice may be won—for instance, to legalize gay marriage, but overall the war is still being won by those who put profit before people, exploitation over the environment, and who claim states matter more than the people who make them. Sorry to say, but those who believe that others should be led, told or coerced, not inspired, are winning. These cynics are far fewer in number than those who want a better way. But they have the better weapons—political access and the abiding power of money over numbers. And their most powerful weapon is secret—it is our own acquiescence and belief in the immutability of the system.

In her brilliant analysis of the recent financial collapse, and how the irresponsible actions of a tiny number of bankers ruined the livelihoods of millions, the *Financial Times* journalist Gillian Tett offers a compelling hypothesis of how the disaster came about: "In most societies, elites try to maintain their power not simply by garnering wealth, but also by dominating the mainstream ideologies, in terms of both what is said and what is *not* discussed. Social 'silences' serve to maintain power structures, in ways that participants often barely understand themselves let alone plan."[2]

Somehow, the neat logic of neoclassical economics and representative democracy has created a mental cage for our minds, and ambitions. In theory, such systems are ideal; but in practice, their imperfections are ever more evident. And yet the theoretical logic is so often repeated, it is as if an insurmountable wall surrounds our imagination: We can see nothing beyond, and dare not even conceive it. We have been numbed into inaction.

In the current way of things, the blatant selfishness, neglect and cruelty of the few is almost easier to stomach than the feeble apathy of those who claim that nothing better is possible, and that this is just the way things *are*, ordained by unarguable theory if not by some supreme power. This is exactly how the silence is perpetuated; this is exactly how the status quo is maintained.

Such numbed passivity is a denial of our very humanity—and moreover leaves the field empty for the foe. It is inhuman to tolerate the rank and visible suffering of others. To believe the patent false-hood that the few who rule know better than the many is as demean-ing to the rulers as to the ruled. It is pathetic to witness the injustice of the status quo and yet do nothing, however slight, to amend it. Above all, this inaction in the face of inequity and looming crisis is to render ourselves less than we are.

There is thrill in the fight, even if there must also be fear. As Spartacus gloriously put it in the eponymous movie, "I'd rather be here, a free man among brothers, facing a long march and a hard fight, than to be the richest citizen in Rome, fat with food he didn't work for, and surrounded by slaves."

But this adventure will not happen of its own accord.

This book is not proposing a revolution against government, but one in our own attitudes. The individual is the most effective agent in altering their immediate circumstances. Thus, they are the most effective agent, when acting collectively, in effecting global change—in anything. Moreover, action opens a possibility that is strange and unfamiliar, a world without limits: to realize at last fully what one is, what we are as humans. This is not an immutable or logical force that we can simply observe and idly comment upon. It requires summon-ing up our own dark forces, our fear, our hunger, our ideals: It re-quires action.

The alternatives are grim to contemplate. The slow but inevitable decline in state power can be arrested, but only by governments ac-quiring more power, thereby constraining our own freedom and ex-acerbating many of the pernicious trends already here identified. The growing sense of disorder will attract those who offer to calm the stormy waters, proclaiming order and certainty in place of chaos.

Twenty-first-century fascism probably won't look much like twentieth-century fascism. We are too inoculated—one hopes—

against the crude semiotics of the swastika and black shirts and the devastating violence of the Holocaust. It will come in a different form, cleverly argued and convincingly presented. Instead of Nazis gathering in Munich beer halls, it may start on a website, for technology is indifferent to democrats or fascists. Indeed, jihadist terrorists share with twentieth-century European fascists their absolutism and willingness to sacrifice innocent life in the construction of a greater society—and they are not alone in this inhuman calculus. Meanwhile, a new breed emerges of European anti-immigration politicians and their American analogues, with smart suits and whitened teeth. As the disorder grows, so too, inevitably, will emerge those who promise to tame it with authoritarianism and, inevitably but admitted only sotto voce, coercive force.

The choice will become clearer: to cede our voice to those louder, to watch while governments, corporations and criminal networks joust for control, or to join battle for agency over affairs that are rightfully our own.

There is no easy answer to the problems that confront humanity in the twenty-first century; it would be foolish to place our faith in one form of management—government—to solve them. Whether environmental degradation, incipient political violence, economic volatility or a host of other dangers, the evidence is stark of government's waning powers. If others are not to exploit this instability, there is but one alternative: to step in ourselves.

The goal cannot be defined neatly, as a concrete system or a state of affairs. It is instead a method, a process, a means—which is itself an end. And by its nature, no one can define where that process may lead. Critics can paint that blank canvas with nightmares; I can suggest instead a future of cooperation, justice, mutual understanding and a deeper sense of purpose upon this crowded planet. If this path is taken, a vista of possibility may open up, beyond the dull limits of the ideas that today dominate our conception of society and ourselves. The limits are of conventional thought; the possibility is of us, ourselves: the human.

Somewhere along the way, anaesthetized by vacuous but incessant politics, ubiquitous advertising and the flickering screen, we have forgotten that we are at our best in adventure, compassion for others and the aspiration for something greater. When confronted by danger and unfathomable challenge, as we surely are, only then are we truly alive. Words like "meaning," "purpose" and "solidarity" capture a small sense of this richness, but in fact it comprises much, much more. It is nothing less than the human project, lived to the fullest. No longer a life of mere silent acceptance, but instead the imagining and construction of a true and direct democracy of the people, a vibrant but just economy and, with these prizes, a better world.

Even failure is better than acquiescence.

ACKNOWLEDGMENTS

More than a dozen people helped with the research for this book over the five years I spent preparing it. I would like particularly to thank Tait Foster, who gave me a great deal of excellent, prompt and accurate research help.

There were many others who read the book, listened to its ideas and provided suggestions and helpful criticism. Many people, therefore, should share the credit for the book, and I thank them sincerely, while all errors of course remain my own. These people include:

Rob Akam, Ardian Arifaj, Lyle Berman, Lili Birnbaum, Stephanie Blair, John Brademas, Jake Camara, Royston Coppenger, David Cornwell, Joy de Menil, Neill Denny, Anna Dupont, Mark Earls, Susanna Emmet, Nick Fraser, Karl French, Sasha Frere-Jones, Katie Genereux, Ed Harriman, Arya Iranpour, Ian Irvine, Mladen Joksic, Tina Kraja, Jordan Kyle, Alnoor Ladha, Horatia Lawson, Ann Lee, Neil Levine, Andrew Lewis, Professor Catherine Lu, Joshua Marston, Catherine Martin, Charlotte Meyer, Professor Laila Parsons, Vincent Pouliot, Catherine Ross, Clementine Ross, Ivo Ross, Karmen Ross, Oliver Ross, Paddy (Alan) Ross, Victoria (Tori) Rowan, Jeffrey Rubin,

ACKNOWLEDGMENTS

Iain Scollay, Imran Shafi, Angharad Thain, Inigo Thomas, Professor Rob Wisnovsky and Melissa Withers.

I want to thank my colleagues at, and the board members of, Independent Diplomat, and Whitney Ellsworth in particular, who have been very patient in tolerating the preparation of this book, and the voluble expression of its ideas, sometimes in very primitive form. I am profoundly grateful to my wife, Karmen, who has accompanied me in the long journey of this book, and remains, as ever, my chief inspiration and most acute critic. More than anyone, she has helped me cut through the wooliness and hypocrisies of political convention, including most particularly my own, to the necessary truths of injustice.

I am especially grateful to David Rosenthal at Blue Rider Press for supporting this book, and for his acute advice and criticism, and to Aileen Boyle and other colleagues at Blue Rider, and to Dorian Hastings, for their rapid and sensitive encouragement and support. And I thank my editor at Simon & Schuster (UK), Mike Jones, who shepherded the book when it must have seemed a doomed venture. I'm deeply indebted to my agents in the UK and U.S., respectively Jonny Geller at Curtis Brown and George Lucas at Inkwell Management. Without their help and encouragement, at times in dark days, this book would not have come into being.

You will find further discussion of this book and other topics, particularly foreign policy, at my personal website, www.carneross.com and by following me on Twitter—@carneross.

You can see more about Independent Diplomat at www.independent diplomat.org. Independent Diplomat is a nonprofit diplomatic advisory group, and a registered 501(c)(3).

NOTES

Introduction: The Sheer Cliff Face

1. "The Flash Crash: Autopsy," *Economist*, Oct. 7, 2010.
2. Alex Evans of Chatham House originated this term.
3. "Food and Water Driving 21st-Century African Land Grab," *Observer*, Mar. 7, 2010.
4. "Immeasurable Loss," *Economist*, Nov. 12, 2008.
5. As reported in *Financial Times*, Nov. 9, 2010.
6. State Department Assistant Secretary for Human Rights Mike Posner, reported in "Clinton Defends Human Rights Approach," *New York Times*, Dec. 14, 2009.
7. Colum Lynch, "U.N. Takes Stock of Its Diminished Influence," Sept. 13, 2010; http://turtlebay.foreignpolicy.com/posts/2010/09/13/un_takes_stock_of_its_diminished_influence.
8. Parag Khanna, "Future Shock: Welcome to the New Middle Ages," *Financial Times*, Dec. 29, 2010.
9. Timothy Garton Ash, "Timothy Garton Ash in Davos: Illiberal Capitalism and New World Disorder," Jan. 28, 2011; available at http://www.b92.net/eng/insight/opinions.php?yyyy=2011&mm=01&nav_id=72392.
10. "Climate Change Diplomacy: Back from the Brink," *Economist*, Dec. 16, 2010.
11. "As Jobs Fade Away," *Economist*, May 6, 2010.

12. Bob Diamond, the chief executive of Barclays Bank, said, "There was a period of remorse and apology; that period needs to be over." His expected bonus that year was over £3 million.

13. Joseph Rowntree Foundation.

14. "China to Alter Taxes in Attempt to Cut Wealth Gap," *Financial Times*, Apr. 20, 2011.

15. "India's Boom Fails to Feed the Hungry," *Financial Times*, Dec. 23, 2010.

16. *Economist*, May 6, 2010.

17. AFP, "Al-Qaeda Vows to Continue Parcel Bomb Attacks," Nov. 20, 2010.

18. C. J. Chivers, *The Gun* (New York: Simon & Schuster, 2010).

19. *Small Arms Survey* (Geneva: Graduate Institute of International and Development Studies, 2009).

20. Steve Graham, "From Helmand to Merseyside: Unmanned Drones and the Militarization of UK Policing," *Open Democracy*, Sept. 27, 2010; http://www.opendemocracy.net/ourkingdom/steve-graham/from-helmand-to-merseyside-military-style-drones-enter-uk-domestic-policing.

21. Dana Priest and William M. Arkin, "Monitoring America" and "Top Secret America," *Washington Post*, Dec. 20, 2010; http://projects.washingtonpost.com/top-secret-america/articles/monitoring-america.

22. Mark Easton, "Life in UK 'Has Become Lonelier,'" BBC website, http://news.bbc.co.uk/2/hi/uk/7755641.stm; see Mark Easton's blog.

23. See http://blogs.census.gov/censusblog/2010/11/index.html, and John T. Cacioppo and William Patrick, *Loneliness: Human Nature and the Need for Social Connection* (New York: Norton, 2008).

1. The Wave and the Suicide Bomber

1. "Iraq Warns of More Suicide Missions," BBC website, Mar. 29, 2003.

2. Dexter Filkins, *The Forever War* (New York: Vintage Books, 2008).

3. BBC website, Apr. 5, 2003; http://news.bbc.co.uk/2/hi/middle_east/2917107.stm.

4. See, for example, Robert Pape, "Suicide Terrorism and Democracy," Cato Institute, Policy Analysis No. 582, Nov. 1, 2006, and other such arguments by Pape.

5. See, for instance, Assaf Moghadam, "Motives for Martyrdom: Al Qaida, Salafi Jihad, and the Spread of Suicide Attacks," *International Security* 33:3, 2009.

6. The PKK in Turkey fights for a Kurdish homeland.

7. Max Hastings, *Retribution: The Battle for Japan 1944–45* (New York: Vintage, 2009).

8. See "Setback for U.S. Mortgage Sector," *Financial Times*, April 30, 2010, quoting a study of that date, Kellogg School of Management, Northwestern University.

NOTES

9. "A Framework for Pro-environmental Behaviors," Department for Environment, Food and Rural Affairs (DEFRA), 2008; http://www.defra.gov.uk/evidence/social/behavior/pdf/behaviors-jan08-report.pdf.

10. Kees Keizer, Siegwart Lindenberg and Linda Steg, "The Spreading of Disorder," *Science Express*, Nov. 20, 2008.

11. Brooks Barnes, "Claudette Colvin: From Footnote to Fame in Civil Rights History," *New York Times*, Nov. 26, 2009.

12. David J. Garrow, quoted in Barnes, "Claudette Colvin: From Footnote to Fame in Civil Rights History."

2. The Pact

1. The picture can be found online at www.nytimes.com/interactive/2008/08/28/us/politics/20080828_OBAMA_PANO.html?scp=2&sq=obama%20denver%20speech&st=cse.

2. OpenSecrets.org.

3. *Morning Edition*, NPR, Feb. 9, 2009.

4. Robert Putnam, *Bowling Alone: The Collapse and Revival of American Community* (New York: Simon & Schuster, 2001).

5. Horst Schlämmer, a mock politician played by a well-known German comedian.

6. "Before Election, Not a Voter Was Stirring," *New York Times*, Aug. 20, 2009.

7. OpenSecrets.org.

8. "The Road to Riches Is Called K Street," *Washington Post*, June 22, 2005.

9. "How BP Drafted Brussels' Climate Legislation," www.Spinwatch.org, Dec. 15, 2010.

10. This trend is well documented in many democratic systems. See, for instance, Peter Mair and Ingried van Biezen, "Party Membership in Twenty European Democracies: 1980–2000," *Party Politics*, Jan. 2001; Robert Putnam, *Democracies in Flux: The Evolution of Social Capital in Contemporary Society* (New York: Oxford University Press, 2002); and most recently, Paul Whiteley, "Is the Party Over? The Decline of Party Activism and Membership across the Democratic World," paper presented at University of Manchester conference, April 2009.

11. The source is worldpublicopinion.org, whose survey "World Public Opinion on Democracy," a twenty-country global public opinion poll on democracy and governance, found that in every nation polled, publics support the principles of democracy. At the same time, in nearly every nation, majorities are dissatisfied with how responsive their government is to the will of the people. For a more detailed analysis, see: http://www.worldpublicopinion.org/pipa/articles/home_page/482.php?lb=hmpg1&pnt=482&nid=&id=.

12. "Cuomo Accepts Millions from the Interests He Assails," *New York Times*, June 23, 2010.

13. Senator Fritz Hollings, interviewed by Bill Moyers on *Bill Moyers Journal*, July 25, 2008; http://www.pbs.org/moyers/journal/07252008/transcript3.html.

14. Center for Responsive Politics.

15. See Nina Bernstein, "City of Immigrants Fills Jail Cells with Its Own," *New York Times*, Dec. 27, 2008.

16. One of the clients of The Gabriel Company, headed by Edward Gabriel, former U.S. ambassador to Morocco is, of course, Morocco. U.S. Department of Justice, Foreign Agents Registration Act (FARA) listings.

17. "American Lobbyists Work for Ivorian Leader," *New York Times*, Dec. 23, 2010.

18. "U.S. Approved Trade with Blacklisted Nations," *New York Times*, Dec. 23, 2010.

19. "While Warning About Fat, U.S. Pushes Cheese Sales," *New York Times*, Nov. 6, 2010.

20. *Private Eye*, Mar. 18, 2011.

21. "Some Philanthropists Are No Longer Content to Work Quietly," *New York Times*, Nov. 7, 2008.

22. Urban Institute, National Center for Charitable Statistics.

23. Grant Jordan and William Maloney, "The Rise of Protest Business in Britain," in J. W. van Deth, ed., *Private Groups and Public Life* (New York: Routledge, 1997).

24. "At National Review, a Threat to Its Reputation for Erudition," *New York Times*, Nov. 17, 2008.

25. "The Daily Me," *New York Times*, Mar. 19, 2009.

26. "The Big Sort," *Economist*, June 19, 2008.

3. Anarchy = Chaos

1. I was the strategy coordinator at the UN Mission in Kosovo (UNMIK) from 2003 to 2004.

2. Human Rights Watch, www.hrw.org.

3. Fareed Zakaria, "What America Has Lost: It's Clear We Overreacted to 9/11," *Newsweek*, Sept. 4, 2010.

4. Rebecca Solnit, *A Paradise Built in Hell: The Extraordinary Communities That Arise in Disaster* (New York: Viking, 2009).

5. Letter from Professor Robert H. Wade, *Financial Times*, Jan. 4, 2010.

6. "From Behind Bars, Madoff Spins His Story," *Financial Times*, Apr. 8, 2011.

7. SEC, Office of Inspector-General Report, case number OIG-509; http://www.sec.gov/spotlight/secpostmadoffreforms/oig-509-exec-summary.pdf.

NOTES

8. See, for instance, "Report Details How Madoff's Web Ensnared S.E.C.," *New York Times*, Sept. 3, 2009.

9. "Chief Regulator Resigns after Strong Criticism," *Financial Times,* May 28, 2010.

10. online.wsj.com/public/resources/documents/MarkopolosTestimony20090203.pdf.

11. Joe Nocera, "Madoff Had Accomplices: His Victims," *New York Times*, Mar. 13, 2009.

12. The full name of the bill is the "Wall Street Reform and Consumer Protection Act of 2009."

13. "Wall Street to Sidestep Volcker Rule," *Financial Times*, Nov. 10, 2010.

14. Letter from Professor Anat Admati of Stanford University and nineteen others, "Healthy Banking System Is the Goal, Not Profitable Banks," *Financial Times*, Nov. 9, 2010.

15. Clive Crook, "We Have Failed to Muffle the Banks," *Financial Times*, Sept. 12, 2010.

16. "Dimon Warns of Bank 'Nail in Coffin,'" *Financial Times*, March 30, 2011.

17. "The Bipartisanship Racket," *New York Times*, Dec. 19, 2010.

18. See Gary Wolf, "Why Craig's List Is Such a Mess," *Wired*, Aug. 24, 2009.

19. Mark Pesce at the Personal Democracy Forum, New York City, 2008.

20. The Business and Human Rights Council is one example.

21. www.sourcemap.org.

22. "From Behind Bars, Madoff Spins His Story," *Financial Times,* Apr. 8, 2011.

23. That NGO is International Crisis Group, whose local researcher, Ardian Arifaj, contributed to the preparation of this section; see the full Crisis Group report on the 2004 violence at www.crisisgroup.org.

24. Eight Serbs and eleven Albanians were killed in the violence; International Crisis Group.

25. Kosovo became a state on February 17, 2008. Independent Diplomat has advised various of its governments and the multiparty negotiating team in this process.

4. The Importance of Meeting People

1. Anthony Beevor, *The Battle for Spain: The Spanish Civil War 1936–1939* (London: Weidenfeld & Nicolson, 2006).

2. www.notonourwatchproject.org.

3. Edmund Sanders, "Is the Darfur Bloodshed Genocide? Opinions Differ," *Los Angeles Times*, May 4, 2009.

4. Rob Crilly has made this accusation in his book *Saving Darfur, Everyone's Favourite African War* (London: Reportage Press, 2010); see also: http://news.bbc.co.uk/go/pr/fr/-/2/hi/africa/8501526.stm.

5. The laughably named lordsoftheblog.net.

NOTES

6. "Chinese Communist Party Opens Online Forum," *Financial Times*, Sept. 14, 2010, including quotation from Russell Leigh Moses, a Beijing-based political analyst.

7. "Athens on the Net," *New York Times*, Sept. 13, 2009.

8. www.seeclickfix.com.

9. "Nigeria Text Messages 'Fuelled Jos Riots.'" BBC News website, January 27, 2010. http://news.bbc.co.uk/2/hi/8482666.stm.

10. Alan Boswell, "Sudan's Government Crushed Protests by Embracing Internet," McClatchy Newspapers, Apr. 7, 2011.

11. "China's Censors Tackle and Trip over the Internet," *New York Times*, Apr. 7, 2010.

12. At the Personal Democracy Forum, New York City, June 2010.

13. Jeffrey Rosen, "Google's Gatekeepers," *New York Times*, Nov. 30, 2008.

14. "The Daily Me," *New York Times*, Mar. 19, 2009.

15. "U.S. Warns of Terror Groups' Western Recruits," *Financial Times*, Oct. 6, 2010.

16. See www.americaspeaks.org: "Unified New Orleans Plan"; this site also has many other examples of deliberative democracy in action.

17. Cass Sunstein, *Going to Extremes: How Like Minds Unite and Divide* (New York: Oxford University Press, 2009); Sunstein is now an adviser to the Obama White House.

18. "How to Get a Better Informed European Public," *Financial Times*, June 3, 2009.

19. A senior Labour government minister, Peter Hain, for instance, chose *Homage* as "the book that changed my life," in the *New Statesman*.

20. George Orwell, *Homage to Catalonia* (Boston: Houghton Mifflin Harcourt, 2010), p. 104.

5. The Man in the White Coat

1. Arendt coined the term, in describing Nazi Adolf Eichmann during his trial: "the banality of evil."

2. Christopher Browning, *Ordinary Men: Reserve Police Battalion 101 and the Final Solution in Poland* (New York: Harper Perennial, 1993).

3. Benedict Carey, "Decades Later, Still Asking: Would I Pull That Switch," *New York Times*, July 1, 2008.

4. Dr. Jerry M. Burger, "Replicating Milgram: Would People Still Obey Today?" *American Psychologist*, Jan. 2009.

5. Professor Joy Gordon, *Invisible War: The United States and the Iraq Sanctions* (Cambridge, Mass.: Harvard University Press, 2010).

NOTES

6. Why Chess Is an Inappropriate Metaphor

1. International Maritime Bureau.
2. See, for instance, Alan Beattie, "Wealthy Countries Fail to Hit Aid Target," *Financial Times*, Feb., 16, 2010.
3. "Millennium Goals" (editorial), *Financial Times*, Sept. 21, 2010.
4. Full title *De la manière de négocier avec les souverains, de l'utilité des negotiations, du choix des ambassadeurs et des envoyez, et des qualitez necessaries pour réussir dans ces employs.*
5. Unpublished research by Independent Diplomat.
6. By contrast, an excellent account of the review conference is online: Rebecca Johnson, "NPT: Challenging the Nuclear Powers' Fiefdom," June 15, 2010; http://www.opendemocracy.net/5050/rebecca-johnson/npt-challenge-to-nuclear-powers-fiefdom.
7. See Alexander Golts, "An Illusory New START," *Moscow Times*, Mar. 30, 2010.
8. EastWest Institute, "Re-framing Nuclear De-Alert: Decreasing the Operational Readiness of U.S. and Russian Arsenals," 2009; http://iis-db.stanford.edu/pubs/22775/reframing_dealert.pdf.
9. Reported in *ScienceDaily*, Dec. 11, 2006, from the annual meeting of the American Geophysical Union in San Francisco, where twin papers on this topic by scientists from Rutgers University, the University of Colorado at Boulder, and the University of California at Los Angeles were announced.
10. Ayman al-Zawahiri, *The Exoneration: A Treatise on the Exoneration of the Nation of the Pen and Sword of the Denigrating Charge of Being Irresolute and Weak* (2008), referred to in Rolf Mowatt-Larssen, "Al Qaeda's Nuclear Ambitions," *Foreign Policy,* Nov. 16, 2010.
11. See Seymour Hersh, "The Online Threat: Should We Be Worried About Cyber War?" *New Yorker*, Nov. 1, 2010.
12. See Niall Ferguson, "Complexity and Collapse: Empires on the Edge of Chaos," *Foreign Affairs,* Mar./Apr. 2010.
13. Professor Page teaches complexity theory at the University of Michigan and presents the invaluable primer on complexity theory, "Understanding Complexity," a DVD-based course from The Teaching Company.
14. See www.commonsecurityclub.org.
15. See, for instance, wevegottimetohelp.org.

7. The Means Are the Ends

1. http://en.wikipedia.org/wiki/Satyagraha, citing M. K. Gandhi, *Satyagraha in South Africa* (Ahmedabad: Navajivan, 1928), pp. 109–10.

NOTES

2. http://en.wikipedia.org/wiki/Dharasana_Satyagraha, citing journalist Webb Miller.
3. Judith Brown, the eminent historian of Gandhi, reaches a more nuanced view of the Salt Satyagraha, and indeed Gandhi's movement of civil resistance, in her excellent essay "Gandhi and Civil Resistance in India, 1917–47," in Adam Roberts and Timothy Garton Ash, eds., *Civil Resistance and Power Politics* (New York: Oxford University Press, 2009). The essay is well worth reading for those interested in judgments of the effectiveness of Gandhi's methods.
4. Ernesto "Che" Guevara, *Guerrilla Warfare* (New York: Penguin Books, 1961).
5. http://en.wikipedia.org/wiki/Zapatista_Army_of_National_Liberation, citing Alain Gresh, "The Dream of a Better World Is Back," *Le monde diplomatique*, May 8, 2009.
6. The POLISARIO Front, the political representatives of the Sahrawi people, is a client of Independent Diplomat.
7. Nelson Santos, East Timor's permanent representative to the United Nations, in conversation with the author.
8. "Group of Bed-Stuy Men, We Make Us Better, Escorts Pedestrians in Wake of Robberies," New York *Daily News*, Nov. 30, 2010.
9. Guy Dinmore, "Naples Fights to Reclaim the Mafia Badlands," *Financial Times*, Sept. 27, 2010.
10. Raghuram G. Rajan, *Fault Lines: How Hidden Fractures Still Threaten the World Economy* (Princeton, N.J.: Princeton University Press, 2010).
11. Transcript and recording available at www.johnlewispartnership.co.uk.
12. "Case Study: How to Cope with a Slump in Demand," *Financial Times*, Dec. 23, 2010.
13. See the review of Kotlikoff's book: Martin Sandbu, "A Less Wonderful Life for Bankers," *Financial Times*, Mar. 22, 2010.
14. See Elinor Ostrom's excellent "meta-research" article "A Behavioral Approach to the Rational Choice Theory of Collective Action: Presidential Address, American Political Science Association, 1997," *American Political Science Review* 92(1): 1–22.
15. The Heritage Foundation published an interesting but not comprehensive analysis of principles to observe in health care cooperatives: Edmund Haislmaier, Dennis Smith and Nina Owcharenko, "Healthcare Cooperatives, Doing It the Right Way," June 18, 2009, available at http://www.heritage.org/research/reports/2009/06/health-care-co-operatives-doing-it-the-right-way.
16. ForestEthics.org.
17. www.cdproject.net.
18. "Banks Grow Wary of Environmental Risks," *New York Times*, Aug. 30, 2010.
19. See, for instance, the Business and Human Rights Resource Centre at www.business-humanrights.org, or www.climatecounts.org.

NOTES

20. This is a paraphrasing of what Bernard-Henri Lévy said during a discussion at the New York Public Library on Sept. 16, 2008. It's possible that I recorded this statement incorrectly, in which case my apologies to the reader and "BHL."

8. Kill the King! Nine Principles to Guide Action

1. If in doubt about this question, please consult my testimony to the Butler inquiry in 2004, and to the Chilcot inquiry in 2010, both available at relevant websites, or upon request.
2. Peter Singer, *The Life You Can Save: Acting Now to End World Poverty* (New York: Random House, 2009).
3. Robert D. Putnam, "*E Pluribus Unum*: Diversity and Community in the 21st Century," 2006 Johan Skytte Prize Lecture, in *Scandinavian Political Studies* 30:2, 2007.
4. You will find further discussion of these options on my personal website, www .carneross.com, and in my opinion article "Let's Boycott, Isolate and Sabotage Gaddafi," *Financial Times*, Mar. 10, 2011.
5. See "Dutch Bankers' Bonuses Axed by People Power," *Observer*, Mar. 27, 2011.
6. See "Helping Women Fight Back Against Street Harassment, Seconds After It Occurs," *New York Times*, Nov. 8, 2010.
7. See this invaluable article on Stuxnet: Michael Joseph Gross, "A Declaration of Cyber-War," *Vanity Fair*, Apr. 2011.

9. Conclusion: A Vision of the Human

1. Quotations from Leo Tolstoy, *War and Peace*, are from the Louise and Aylmer Maude translation (New York: Macmillan, 1943).
2. Gillian Tett, *Fool's Gold: The Inside Story of J. P. Morgan and How Wall St. Greed Corrupted Its Bold Dream and Created a Financial Catastrophe* (New York: Free Press, 2009).

INDEX

INDEX

INDEX

INDEX

INDEX

INDEX

INDEX

INDEX

Political extremism
  democracy and, 105
  European Parliament elections and,
    104–5
  interest groups and, 57
Political influence, 47–48
Political insecurity, rise of, 12–16
Political theories, and interconnected age, 6
Politicians
  chasm between voters and, 46 47
  deepening divide between citizens and, 58
  disrespect toward, 46, 48–49
  lobbyists and, 47, 48, 49, 50–57
  problem with, xv
  problem solving of, 7–8, 20–22
  rule of politics by elites, executives and,
    47
  See also Politics
Politics
  change and, 18–19
  decisions divorced from voter needs,
    51–54, 57
  disrespect toward, 46, 48–49
  elites, executives and politicians, rule of,
    47
  health compromised by, 53–54
  ineffectiveness of, 18–19
  Internet and, 94–96
  of meeting people, 101
  money in, 49–50, 54, 55
  new-world requirement of new, 8
  problems and, 18–19
  reclaiming agency in, 89, 216
  watching instead of acting on, 45
  See also British politics; U.S. politics
Polling, 107. See also Deliberative polling
Ponzi scheme
  classic sign of, 73
  Madoff, 68–74, 82–84
Porto Alegre experiment, 102–3, 168
Poverty, 136, 185, 186, 187
Power
  adaptation to new technology, 98
  globalization and shifts in, 7

government, 215
  leaderless revolution philosophy of
    reclaiming, xxv
  monopolization in democracies, xv
  See also Action; Agency
Private companies, 210
  health insurance, 174–75, 176
  model of workplace, xxi–xxii
Private ownership, and common resources,
  174
Problems
  agency as answer to, 18
  escape from overwhelming, 17
  of globalization, 8
  inaction, detachment and polarization in
    reaction to, 22
  intractable, 17–18
  politics and, 18–19
Problem solving
  of anarchism, 23
  through collective decision making, 23
  of governments, 8–10, 20–22
  new method of, xvii
  of politicians, 7–8, 20–22
Protests, 165, 208, 209, 213. See also Arab
    spring; Occupy Wall Street protests
    and movement
Public provision vs. private ownership of
    common resources, 174. See also
    Citizens
"Pursuit of the Ideal, The" (Berlin),
    107–8
Putnam, Robert, 16, 189, 190

Ramanand, Sant, 1–2
Regulation
  attempt to prevent future economic
    crash (2010), 75–78
  bank, xvi, 77, 137
  failure, 70–74, 75–78, 82, 83–84
  financial industry, 74, 75–78, 82, 83
  investment industry, 69, 70, 71, 72,
    73–74, 75–78, 82, 83, 137
  oil industry, 71

INDEX

Regulation (*cont.*)
  problem with, 75
  Wall Street, 75–78, 83
Representative democracy, 214
  alternatives to, xxvi
  anarchy and, 89
  decision making and, xviii–xix, 106–7
  deliberative polling and, 107, 108
  evolution from direct to, 46–47
  incompatibility of deliberative
        democracy and, 106–7, 108
  political change and, 42, 46
Representative democracy pact, 43–45,
        58–59
  breakdown of, 45–47, 58, 59
Representatives. *See* Politicians
Revolution, 208–9
  of attitudes, 215
  Communists on, 177
  Internet as, 89
  violent, 212
  See also Leaderless revolution
Riots, Kosovo, 61–65, 85–86, 87, 88
Russia, 3, 152, 154. *See also* Soviet Union

Sabotage, 199–200
Salt tax and Salt March, 159–63, 193
Satyagraha (holding firm to truth), 160,
        161, 162
Saudi Arabia, 3, 132
Securities and Exchange Commission
        (SEC), 70–71, 72, 73, 74, 82, 83,
        85
Securities industry. *See* Investment industry
Segregation on buses, U.S., 36–37, 198
Self, change of, 23. *See also* Individuals
Self-organization
  international affairs and, 148
  in leaderless revolution philosophy, xxv
  See also Anarchism
Self-organized government, 59–60
  anarchism as, 59–60, 111
  creation of, 212–13
  international, 213

September 11, 2001, attacks, 4, 31,
        132
Shaming, public, 198–99
Singer, Peter, 186, 187, 188
SNCC. *See* Student Nonviolent
        Coordinating Committee
Social change, 37. *See also* Change
Social influence of mimicry, 32–34
Social media, xviii
  Arab spring and, 97, 183–84
  negative uses of, 97
Somalia, 133–34
Soviet Union, 4, 28, 181. *See also* Russia
Spanish Civil War
  anarchism during, 91–92, 109,
        110–11
  Communist suppression of anarchists in,
        109–10, 207
  fight against fascism, 110, 111
  Orwell and, 91–92, 110–11
Stadium wave, 31–32, 34–36, 155
States
  dissociation from people's needs, 138,
        139–41
  identification of diplomats with, 140
  identification of governments with,
        142
  interests, 68, 139–40, 213
  system of international affairs, 140–48,
        213
  See also Governments
Stirner, Max, 186–87, 188
Strikes
  Homestead, Pennsylvania (1892),
        195–97
  hunger, 164–65, 166
Student asylum, from repressive regimes,
        181–82
Student Nonviolent Coordinating
        Committee (SNCC), 166
Stuxnet computer worm, 200
Subprime mortgage crisis, 4, 5, 74, 75
Subprime mortgage defaults, 4, 5
Sudan, 93–94, 97–98

INDEX